Aeschylus
Plays: One

Persians
Seven Against Thebes
Suppliants
Prometheus Bound

The four tragedies included in this volume and the three
which comprise the *Oresteia* (to be found in *Aeschylus Plays:
Two*) are the only ones to have survived of some ninety
plays Aeschylus is reputed to have written. He created a
forum for public and private debate and developed a means
and a concrete stage language for demonstrating that debate
to his own and subsequent generations. Few dramatists
could make such a claim to all-embracing authority.

These sharp and speakable translations by Frederic Raphael
and Kenneth McLeish are complemented by historically
illuminating introductions by the translators and the series
editor, J Michael Walton.

This is a companion volume to *Aeschylus Plays: Two*, which
includes the *Oresteia: Agamemnon, Libation-Bearers* and
Eumenides.

Aeschylus, the first of the Greek dramatists whose work has
survived, was born at Eleusis near Athens in c525BC of
reputedly aristocratic parents. He began his theatrical
career in his twenties, and wrote, directed and acted in
some ninety plays. He fought at the battles of Marathon in
490BC and Salamis in 480BC against the Persians. In later
life he visited Sicily, where some of his plays may have been
first performed, and he died there in 456BC.

AESCHYLUS

Plays: One
introduced by J Michael Walton

Persians
Seven Against Thebes
Suppliants
Prometheus Bound

translated by Frederic Raphael and
Kenneth McLeish

series editor: J Michael Walton

METHUEN DRAMA

METHUEN'S WORLD DRAMATISTS

These translations first published in Great Britain in 1991 by
Methuen Drama, Michelin House, 81 Fulham Road, London
SW3 6RB and distributed in the United States of America by
HEB Inc., 361 Hanover Street, Portsmouth, New Hampshire
NH 03801 3959.

ISBN 0-413-65190-8

A CIP catalogue record for this book is available from the
British Library.

*The painting on the front cover is House + Light + Sky (Maisons
+ lumières + ciel) by Luigi Russolo (1912/13). Permission has
kindly been given by Oeffentliche Kunstsammlung Basel,
Kunstmuseum. Transparency from Colorphoto Hans Hinz. The
back cover shows Aeschylus, from the Farnese Collection, National
Museum, Naples.*

*Typeset by Saxon Printing Ltd, Derby
Printed and bound in Great Britain
by Cox & Wyman Ltd, Cardiff Road, Reading*

Caution

CONTENTS

EDITOR'S INTRODUCTION

Aeschylus wrote as many as ninety plays. The titles of most of them have survived, but – apart from the four included in the present volume and the three which comprise the *Oresteia* – little else. Some fragments (none longer than 20 lines) and a number of quotations in later writers are the only primary support for these seven plays on which Aeschylus' reputation is based. Even to describe them as 'seven plays' is misleading, because Aeschylus created plays not singly but in groups. *Persians*, *Suppliants* and *Seven Against Thebes* were parts of tetralogies whose other plays do not survive; *Prometheus Bound* (if it is by Aeschylus at all – see page xxxii) was one of a linked pair of plays. The three parts of the *Oresteia* (*Agamemnon*, *Libation-Bearers*, *Eumenides*) reveal how dependent any single play in a group could be upon the others. And even the *Oresteia*, complete as it may seem, is incomplete: its satyr play *Proteus*, fourth in the sequence, is missing.

To describe Aeschylus as having 'written' plays can be equally misleading. Direct information about the theatre of his time is meagre, but there seems little doubt that he involved himself centrally in every stage of the process of creating a stage work, from conception to performance (see page xv). Few subsequent dramatists could make such a claim to all-embracing authority. To Aeschylus the Western world owes the double benefit of creating a forum for public and private debate, and simultaneously developing a means and a concrete stage language for demonstrating that debate to his own and subsequent generations.

'History' had no mouthpiece for the ancient Greeks prior to Herodotus, who was probably eight years old when Aeschylus presented his 'historical' play *Persians* in 472BC. The Greeks, and notably the Athenians, were aware of the past but lived in the present. Certain landmarks were fixed in their consciousness: the expulsion of the last tyrant, for example, or the victories over the Persians at Marathon and at Salamis. Past events might be dated from as early as the first

Olympiad in 776BC, but any analysis of the past relied less on actual happenings and specific people than on a body of myth one of whose chief virtues was its flexibility.

In surviving Greek tragedy *Persians* is unique in dealing, albeit in a fictionalised form, with the recent past and with characters who were known, if only by name, to the entire first audience. Elsewhere in the extant plays of Aeschylus, Sophocles and Euripides, there are no 'real' people. The characters are from myth: Agamemnon, Odysseus and Hecuba come from the Trojan cycle; Pentheus, Oedipus and Antigone come from the Theban cycle; and from the deeper past come such characters as Prometheus, Ocean and Danaus. Through many of the stories the Olympian gods and ubiquitous individuals like Heracles travel across time and location with no concern for the mass of apparent inconsistencies. Theseus is a typical figure: a legendary king of Athens who probably did live but who, like Arthur of the Britons, has greater literary and historical potential as a fluid character than as a formed individual.

Something of the sort could be said of every other character in ancient tragedy. The outlines of their fates are fixed, but as individuals they can constantly be renewed through a playwright's versatility. Aeschylus, Sophocles and Euripides each wrote an Electra play. Each wrote a *Philoctetes* and an *Oedipus*, though only those of Sophocles survive. These various plays placed the familiar figures in different situations, a change of detail resulting in a novel emphasis. For example – to take just one small point – in Aeschylus' *Seven Against Thebes* Oedipus' sons Eteocles and Polynices are regarded as twins; in Euripides' *Phoenician Women*, by contrast, Eteocles is the elder, while in Sophocles' *Oedipus at Colonus* he is the younger who has usurped the throne by throwing out Polynices. The moral issues change accordingly. The individual vision of Aeschylus relates to his creating specific circumstances, whether deep in the past or close to home, in order to enlighten and teach in a society that was undergoing the most fundamental intellectual, social and political change.

Before Aeschylus was born, Pisistratus, sole ruler of Athens for most of the period 561-527BC, had instituted or developed a number of state festivals, amongst them the Great Dionysia at which, alongside various rites and sacrifices for the god Dionysus, there were dance competitions and recitations of the Homeric epics. Though the recitation of such poems was doubtless dramatic and possibly involved musical and choral accompaniment, it was not until shortly before the birth of Aeschylus (c525BC) that a new form, tragedy, developed from a combination of choral and oral tradition. The Athenian indifference to the specifics of their past leaves much of the process and timing in the realms of speculation, but the new form featured a Chorus and, for the first time, an actor, both masked. Two hundred years later, Aristotle claimed in the *Poetics* that 'tragedy developed by degrees, went through a number of changes and stopped when it acquired its true nature'. Some of the detail he appends to this bald statement is more helpful, for example when he identifies tragedy as having originated in a cyclic dance known as the dithyramb, and states that Aeschylus increased the number of actors from one to two, subordinating the Chorus 'in favour of dialogue'.

Such prescriptive statements, by someone who was not a practitioner of drama, are not accepted by all scholars, or at their face value. The present translators, for example, on pages xvi-xxiii of this volume and in their Introduction to Volume Two, advocate large pinches of salt. Nonetheless, somewhere between a festival of dance and recitation and a festival featuring the plays of Aeschylus came the moment of transformation when, for the first time, someone impersonated (as opposed to imitated) a character in a story. Almost certainly that moment coincided with the first wearing of the mask. Out of it came the concept of the first actor. Such an innovation is variously described in later sources, none of which can be regarded as authoritative. From the possible claimants to the title of 'inventor of tragedy', the best case is made for Thespis (who won the first-ever drama prize in Athens, in the 530s BC). Although Aristotle never mentions him, his name heads a list of prizewinners (now known as the Parian Marble), and the comic playwright Aristophanes, in his play *Wasps* of 422BC, refers to a character 'dancing those old dances with which Thespis used to compete'. (This would appear a conclusive enough early reference were it not for a later commentator's note in the manuscript saying that the reference is to Thespis the harpist, not Thespis the playwright.)

All details of the earliest manifestations of tragedy are similarly obscure. Small wonder that the theatre historian is usually content to leave linguist to squabble with archaeologist, sociologist with anthropologist, and to accept that the plays of Aeschylus represent a dramatic form which had already undergone some sixty years of experiment and growth prior to the presentation of *Persians* (Aeschylus' first surviving play) in 472BC. Of the playwrights before Aeschylus and of his contemporaries not enough is known to estimate either how innovative he was or what competition he faced. Most are merely names: Choerilus and Pratinas, for example, are as shadowy as Thespis. One, Phrynichus, is interesting for the light he throws on the possible reception of *Persians* at its first production, before an Athenian audience – a majority of whom would have fought in or witnessed the battle of Salamis eight years before – a battle so graphically described by the Persian messenger in the play (see page 13). Some 25 years before *Persians*, Phrynichus' *The Capture of Miletus* had so powerfully reminded the Athenians of an incident they would have preferred to forget (the Persian sack of Miletus in 494BC) that he was impeached and fined. The grief, dismay or guilt which that performance engendered shows unequivocally how effective the theatre could be, and the extent to which a playwright had to balance the function of the theatre to needle and disconcert, with a respect for local sensibilities. Later in the century Euripides and Aristophanes both fell foul of the authorities. Aeschylus himself faced a charge of revealing, if unwittingly, details of the Eleusinian Mysteries.

If few plays offered so direct a message as did *The Capture of Miletus* or *Persians*, the expectations of audiences were clearly geared to emotional impact both at the literal level of the story and as an allegory of contemporary issues. In this, the spoken word was of major importance. A combination of narrative and argument is one feature of the transition from epic to dramatic, but it is certainly not the only feature. Apart from words, the playwright had available a significant arsenal. He had a festival occasion of holiday, reverence and mystery. (What else should theatre be?) He had the open air of a Greek spring when the sights and smells of the world confirm the annual miracle. He had the complex pattern of myth, a history or pseudo-history so rich in figures, in possibilities and alternatives, a boundless world for the imagination, his own and that of his audience. The visual tradition of art, sculpture and pottery stemmed from a growing appreciation of the values of figures and objects in line and space. All round him and every day, people expressed themselves formally, socially and ceremonially through movement and dance; individually, corporately, in earnest and in play. And in an oral poetic tradition he had access to a tested and familiar means of story-telling to create the past, or a series of pasts, as a way to address issues of the present and the future.

The momentous political changes of Aeschylus' lifetime, the movement in Athens from a form of monarchy to a form of democracy, have their counterpart in a move in art away from the static and cumbersome heroism of the sixth century BC to a new sense of personal responsibility. The theatre at Athens was never a place of escape. Drama ran parallel to life. It was an aspect of a world-view; its perspective measured the instinct for survival against the experience of suffering.

The partial experience of that vision which the dearth of surviving plays prescribes, ensures that those we do have are treasured all the more. With the conditions of the first performances overtaken by two and a half thousand years of theatre experience, claims for revival might appear difficult to argue. Today's theatre, though, is a theatre of image, and the power of image, verbally and physically, is the quality in Aeschylus most easy to recognise whether at a reading or in performance. The physical apparatus of his theatre is no better known than the process by which non-dramatic poetry became drama. The sense of space and perspective created as a result of the angle of viewing in performing areas such as the Theatre of Dionysus (see page xiv) affords a rich picture of a theatre developing and changing in its physical and emotional range. The apparently static structure of many scenes in

Aeschylus combines the rhythm of contrast with the power of economy. 'In the theatre,' as Sir Peter Hall once said, commandeering a phrase of the architect Mies Van Der Rohe, 'less is more'. When Euripides, as a character in Aristophanes' *Frogs*, mocks Aeschylus for his static figures, majestic silences and spectacular effects, he gives licence to future generations to recognise and acknowledge Aeschylus' sense of stage-picture. The surviving plays, few as they are, offer proof of the poet and the thinker. Equally clearly they show an artist who may not have discovered a new art-form, but who first enabled it to demonstrate a potential to which every subsequent playwright owes allegiance.

TRANSLATORS' INTRODUCTION

Aeschylus

Although evidence is sparse for the early years of Greek (that is, Athenian) drama, scholars generally agree that it had been a recognisable genre for perhaps a generation before Aeschylus began to write. Performances took place in honour of Dionysus, in the earliest days in the Agora, and by Aeschylus' time in the god's shrine at the foot of the Acropolis. Their essence was probably choral movement and song, perhaps with a single solo actor/singer, and the basic material was usually drawn from myth. There was a second, supposedly older and certainly shadowier tradition, of myth-burlesques featuring a chorus of satyrs, the goat-footed followers of Dionysus in his form as Bacchus, lord of intoxication. The first tradition evolved (partly thanks to Aeschylus) into the kinds of 'Greek tragedy' which survive today. The second evolved into the 'satyr play' which usually closed each day's theatrical events, and of which Aeschylus was an acknowledged master.

Aeschylus' surviving plays are all late works: the first of them, *Persians*, was produced when he was 53, with some 25 years' experience. The work of his early years, like that of his older contemporaries Choerilus, Pratinas and Phrynichus (on whom see page x), is known only in sketchy outlines. Later tradition, unsupported by evidence but persistent, claims that he himself introduced many of the innovations which gave tragedy the form and style familiar to us from surviving plays. Whether his or not, two of these innovations were crucial: the introduction of a second actor (allowing a much wider variety of musical style, as well as spoken dialogue not involving the Chorus), and the use of scenery to give precise location to the action.

Other new ideas are less plausibly claimed for Aeschylus. He is said to have pioneered the use of exotic costumes, and to have favoured such elaborate stage effects as flying, thunderstorms and the like. Such attributions, out of keeping with most of what is known of Greek tragedy, may stem more from a reading of Aeschylus' plays (where extravagant events are regularly described) than from independent evidence, and may be the result of scholars, dusty from the study rather than the rehearsal room, taking his words too literally. It is a (malign) form of the suspension of disbelief Shakespeare asks for in the Prologue to *Henry V*.

In his own time, Aeschylus was renowned as a 'teacher' of his audience (he so describes dramatists in Aristophanes' *Frogs*). He used the forms of drama to present and articulate dilemmas of politics, ethics, philosophy and every other aspect of relationships between humans and humans, humans and the supernatural – and then 'cast' his spectators, leaving them to ponder on the issues raised in the theatre in such an uncompromising and stirring form. We discuss this aspect of his art in more detail in our Introduction to the *Oresteia*, his most substantial surviving work. What follows here is a description of the theatrical means available to him, and the uses he made of them.

So far as these means can be reconstructed, they were extremely simple. Aeschylus' plays were performed in a large circular space in the shrine of Dionysus (hub of the later theatre). The audience sat in tiers round the perimeter of the circle. There may have been a stage area along the edge of the circle facing the Acropolis. Performances were part of an annual festival (the Great Dionysia: see page ix), and were competitive. On each day of the festival, a (male) Chorus of 12, with two or three (male) actors and a handful of non-speaking extras, performed three tragedies (sometimes linked) and one satyr play, all by the same author, drawing out themes from religious myth. Each play consisted of choral movement and song (sometimes over half the action), lyric song and dance by the actors (perhaps a quarter of the action) and spoken dialogue between actor and Chorus or actor and actor. If the surviving plays are anything to go by, proportions of lyric to speech varied from play to play, playwright to playwright and generation to generation. By and large, the plays of Sophocles and Euripides contain more speech than lyric; by and large, Aeschylus' choruses bear the main performance 'weight'. Aeschylus' acting-company was probably headed by the playwright himself; he is also thought to have composed the music, directed the plays and super-vised the choreography. (This was common: we are told, for example, that Sophocles had to stop performing in mid-career because of voice-strain. Even so, one wonders how much delegation there was, and for what reasons.)

It is impossible to exaggerate the importance of music in an ancient performance of Aeschylus – an element hard to reconstruct or imagine, since none survives. The verse metres were also those of both music and dance. They consisted of repeated patterns of long and short syllables, balancing or counterpointing the natural stresses of Greek speech. There were over a dozen basic patterns, and the most important had traditional associations. Anapaests, for exam-ple (groups of two short syllables followed by one long one, with the stress on the first short syllable) were used to accompany dignified choral movement (for example process-ing into or out of the theatre). Iambics (one short syllable followed by one long, with the stress on the short syllable) were used for spoken dialogue. More complex rhythmic groups, for example choriambics (long-short-short-long) or epitrites (long-short-long-long), were used for lyric song and dance; the choreographic possibilities are fascinating, though almost entirely speculative. The music was monodic (without harmony), and the singing may have been 'shadowed' (rather than accompanied) by such instruments as oboe, lyre, drum and finger-cymbals. In later times, 'modes' were used: scales, each of which had a particular association (warlike, sad and so on). There is no evidence that they were used in Aeschylus' time. Long choral passages were often divided into patterns of statement and response, the syllable-lengths of one section exactly repeating those of the one before: a device with apparent (though unprovable) implications for staging and performance. Aeschylus' surviving plays are also studded with exclamations: *ee-ay*, *o-toto-to-ee*, *E! E!* (the 'e' short as in 'hen'), *o-ah* and so on. These were probably not transliera-tions of exact sounds, but indications to the performers that particular kinds of melismas or cadenzas were required. (We have left many of them in place in this translation.)

Effects such as these resist translation, not least because heavily rhythmic verse in English tends to sound galumphing rather than musical, hobbling the expression. But they are vital to the construction and progress of an Aeschylean play in Greek, just as patterns of rhythm and expression are to a musician today. Indeed, Aeschylus' construction-methods in several surviving plays can best be understood by musical, rather than literary, analogies: see pages xxv, xxix. He used all the possibilities of syntax-variation in the highly-inflected Greek language: the range is from crisp declarative sentences of two or three words, to elaborate, multi-image constructions of a dozen lines or more. In a similar way his vocabulary ranges from limpid everyday words, to extravagant coinages and metaphor of a boldness no other surviving Greek poet equals. Allusion is a feature of his style: recurring reference to key ideas and images, not developed but dropped in in passing, as it were, reminding us of the context or implications of what we can currently hear or see.

Persians

Persians is unique among extant tragedies in being based on a historical, rather than a mythical, event. The destruction of the Persian invaders in 480BC was, of course, of crucial importance to the Greeks, but it proved 'mythical' only in the sense that it became fundamental to Hellenic self-esteem. The earlier defeat of Darius, at Marathon in 490BC, had been salutary, both militarily and (in particular) for the self-confidence of the Athenians, who had won a land battle without the aid of the procrastinating Spartans. But Darius' expedition had been a reconnaissance in force, whereas that of his son Xerxes, with its massive amphibious operation, was an imperial venture, intended both to punish the Greeks for their past delinquencies and to put their future permanently under Persian control. Aeschylus, it is plausibly claimed, fought at both Marathon and Salamis. His play is certified by its author's participation in what he describes; its genius lies in his empathy with what he imagined to have happened in Persia itself, where he had never been.

Persians was first performed in 472BC. Gilbert Murray suggested (though others have disputed his evidence) that it might have been part of an annual celebration of the Greek victory; the implication is that it was out of the normal tragic run and (having been 'produced', that is financed, by the young Pericles) deserves the compromised status of a commissioned monument rather than that of an autonomous dramatic work. Other aspersions have been cast on its lack of conformity with 'true tragedy' according to Aristotelian or other canons. It seems to have escaped attention that Aeschylus was the source of many tragic 'rules'; his failure to adhere to them is not the symptom of inattention or want of aesthetic consistency. If he failed to observe certain 'laws' of orthodox dramatic construction, so much the worse for orthodoxy, so much the better for drama.

The use of an historical event as the basis of a play was rare in Athenian drama, but not unique. As the present editor has pointed out, Phrynichus, an older contemporary of Aeschylus, was famous – indeed notorious – for his *Siege of Miletus*, in which he depicted the recent capture and sack of Athens' sister city, in Ionia, by the Persians. The Miletans' misfortune was also the Athenians' shame: the latter failed signally to honour their promise to help Miletus against the Great King. When Phrynichus' play moved its audience to tears and even to hysteria, the Athenians did not, in the event, congratulate him on it: he was fined heavily for his tactless rehearsal of a national scandal.

Phrynichus ran no such risk when, shortly before Aeschylus, he wrote a play celebrating a national triumph, the defeat of Xerxes' expedition. We shall never know how closely Aeschylus followed Phrynichus' pattern: the ancient world made no crime of plagiarism nor a fetish of originality. But we may assume that there were similarities – a phrase known to echo Phrynichus may be read as homage – and there are certainly innovations. Whether *Persians* was a 'one-off' or whether – as some scholars maintain – it formed part of a curiously heterogeneous tetralology (of which it alone was 'factual') hardly need concern us. It may be an occasional piece – a sort of hymn of Panhellenic joy – or it may be a chip from a larger block; but in any case it stands alone in the surviving canon.

What kind of play is it, and what kind of achievement? Aeschylus' originality lies in two main and largely unremarked areas. If it is true that his play celebrates a Greek (and in particular an Athenian) triumph, it is also the case that it does so in an unprecedented way: the innovation lies in the negative space defined by the lamentations which fill the stage. In the architecture of the Parthenon (not yet built when the play was completed), the spaces bracketed by the columns resemble amphorae: they have a shaped vacancy, like statues made of air. Not dissimilarly, we have a sense, in this play, through being presented with an account of how appallingly the Persians have failed, of how momentously the Greeks have succeeded. The play may serve a manifest purpose, but it involves an imaginative leap of rare proportions: the audience is made aware of what is *not* discussed, *not* enacted – their own triumph – and also of the danger of pressing it beyond its proper bounds. Celebration and warning are combined. At the Olympic Games of 480BC, the Athenian Themistocles – deviser of the sly trick which Aeschylus' messenger attributes to an anonymous Greek – was cheered by the assembled Hellenes for a *whole day*; at the same time, we are reminded, Persia was in mourning. It is wonderfully appropriate to Aeschylus' wary patriotism that Themistocles himself, ostracised by the Athenians, was to end his days as a Persian satrap. Life, like drama, is full of *peripeteia*, reversal of fortune.

If it is true that Homer, in his presentation (in the *Iliad*) of the Trojans, in particular of Priam's dignity and Hector's conjugal devotion, is the first poet to depict both sides of a war with compassion, it is because, in some sense, both sides subscribe to the same heroic values. It would, in any case, have been absurd (as well as lopsided) to have borne a vengeful grudge against a mythical enemy of the Greeks whose ways were indistinguishable from their own. The Persians, on the other hand, were a very different 'Other'.

They had recently menaced the very existence of Greece; to be accused of 'Medising' – of aping the ways or favouring the hegemony of Persia – was a capital offence of which even a Spartan king (Pausanias) could be accused. And yet Aeschylus decided (possibly on Phrynichus' initiative) to portray Persia's defeat from the Persian point of view, as a 'tragedy' which may have been the consequence of *hubris* but which is depicted in terms of human desolation.

Some scholars have suggested that the dramatised humiliation of Xerxes was intended to be derisory, that it was an invitation for the kind of savage laughter with which even the classical Greeks can be suspected of greeting the pain of a defeated foe. Xerxes' appearance in rags at the end of the play is a sour climax which finds an echo in the kind of Roman triumph in which a beaten enemy – for instance Jugurtha – was paraded in despicable finery at his conqueror's victory procession before being done to death. (Jesus' crown of thorns and shabby purple robe were quite in the Graeco-Roman tradition.) Xerxes' wailing is an instance of 'barbarian' immodesty which earned him bad reports from schoolmasters who advocated the stiff upper lip, but it may be seen, more generously and more plausibly, as the kind of purgative ululation typical of oriental funerals. Its lack of moderation may be an affront to the Apollonian style ('Nothing in excess'), but its very 'self-indulgence' is the ritual prelude to Xerxes' putting the whole disaster behind him. There is no suggestion that Persia will not revive or that the Great King will present no further threat to Greek freedom.

Xerxes' mother, Queen Atossa, is the vessel of a more dignified, if hardly less horrified, response to the disaster of Salamis. As a woman, she might have been expected by the (male) Greek audience to collapse; her unblinking practicality in the face of condign defeat is all the more remarkable. The capacity of Aeschylus and his great successors to vest their sympathy in women, whether villains like Clytemnestra, nay-saying martyrs like Antigone, foreign witches like Medea, or barbarian empresses like Hecuba or Atossa, is evidence of an imaginative leap which 'victims' – for example disenfranchised or disregarded females – can often license in the poetic fancy.

Queen Atossa is not a tragic figure, although she figures in a tragedy. Once again we can detect the negative presence of what she might have been: an instance of derelict majesty. Her refusal to be unhinged by events is the measure both of her own royal character and, in due course, of the disaster which has struck her son. Once again, scholars who seek to invoke some supposed laws of dramatic construction diagnose a flaw in the way in which she leaves the stage (twice) without confronting her son. The obvious 'improvement', they tell us – how full the world is of re-writers! – calls for a reproachful or reconciliatory climax, a tableau involving mother and penitent son. They claim that only Aeschylus' wish (for which there is no evidence) to have both mother and son played by the same actor led him to subtract the Queen from the stage before bringing in Xerxes.

Such arguments miss the point. By the time the Queen departs on the second occasion, in the hope but not the expectation of meeting her son, she has delivered an object lesson in the balanced response to disaster. In this way, her admirable qualities prepare us for the climactic test of her son's resilience. She has illustrated, to perfection, what he proves perfectly incapable of equalling. If she had been present on stage during his arrival (which one can very well imagine, as a dramatic exercise), what purpose might she plausibly have served? Her sympathy might have assuaged Xerxes' pain or her reproaches exasperated and chastened him, but the 'drama' of such a meeting would have socialised Xerxes' isolated anguish before its full expression, in womanish hysteria, proved to what degree men become women, as women can be men, in times of catastrophe. The reversal of roles also offers an implicit judgment on the tyrannous imposture of absolute monarchy, where men-gods who literally cannot be criticised are doomed to be judged by the immortals (who cannot be intimidated like Persian elders).

Although such a conscious 'lesson' was probably never in Aeschylus' mind, dramatic purpose is not inconsistent with ambiguity. The thrust of *Persians* is never merely didactic, but the potential self-destructivenss of violence is a constant theme of the tragedians; the duplicity of Ares, god of war, is never to be forgotten. The Athenian dramatists were, it could be said, to their *polis* what the prophets were to the kings of Israel. Both enjoyed a perilous eminence; fame and disgrace – so they taught, and so they found in their own lives – were two sides of the same coin. Aeschylus the war-hero and cultural ornament narrowly escaped a later charge of impiety which might have carried the death penalty; Phidias, architect of the Parthenon, fled for his life from a similar charge. Artistic eminence could be lonely.

The scholars' other main charges against *Persians* concern what they see as a want of dramaturgical competence. The play is said to be more a vocalised dirge than a proper clash of characters. The Messenger is said to arrive (at the 'wrong' moment) with stale news, since the disaster is already presaged in the opening chorus and would, in any event, be well known to the audience. Such charges attack a dramatist of straw, a material which plays no part in Aeschylus' composition. In their urge to carp, critics have missed here (and elsewhere) a crucial aspect of his genius as a dramatist: his mastery of time. To take another instance: scholars affect to be puzzled by the way in which Xerxes is supposedly wearing the same clothes which he ripped when the battle of Salamis started to go against him. How could he have kept them on for all those weeks or months? In fact it is not implausible to imagine him doing so – the defeated often stumble home in stained dejection – but it is as ridiculous to spend very long on such 'realistic' and wholly inappropriate considerations, as it is to devote pages to deciding precisely where the action of the play's three 'acts' is supposed to take place. Was Aeschylus really 'in error' to put Xerxes' capital and his father's tomb in the same place, although they were hundreds of miles apart?

The simplest response to all this is that dramatists tell a different truth from geographers or gazetteers. A subtler reply would be that the organisation of space in Greek drama is more like that on a vase painting or mural, in which spatial juxtaposition could indicate temporal sequence, than it is like that in an atlas. Beyond this, however, we would argue that Aeschylus was a master of the arrangement of time, adept in its acceleration, in slowing it down or even, as in *Persians*, in

its rehearsal from another perspective. In this respect it is
instructive to refer to cinematic montage, to flashbacks and
flashes forward, to the tricks by which time, rendered
'visual', is arrested or advanced in the interests of narrative
variety and suspense. The absence of surprise by no means
blights suspense; our knowledge does not lessen the slightly
morbid excitement of wondering how the Queen will react
when indubitable news of the Persian disaster reaches her.
The Greek audience is, at it were, in another time zone: its
day is her night, just as her night reminds it of the brilliant
dawn which victory brought, recreating the suspense from
which her defeat dispensed the Greeks.

Once we cease to cavil at Aeschylus' decision not to write
his play as modern authorities on ancient dramatic structure
might prescribe, we are free to honour his adept practice.
Careful reading shows how skilfully he parades the Persian
army, first in its swaggering glory, name by name, like the
stars in some epic folly, and then as an almost endless list of
dishonoured, if not ungallant, casualties. In the same way,
the battle of Plataea, at which the Spartans (in particular)
killed the surviving forces from Salamis, is hinted at before it
is briefly, but terribly, announced. No dramatist can rely on
the audience being able to re-read a page; he or she must
make each point once and for all (or re-present it in a fresh
way each time). Aeschylus, the very inventor of dramatic
forms, constantly contrives solutions for problems which still
arise today: he jumps back and forth in time, making himself
its master and, in the process, eliminating the need for
bridging passages which will allow for temporal plausibility
at the cost of tedium or an unwanted regularity of dramatic
rhythm. By bringing Xerxes 'too quickly' from the Hellespont to his palace, in the space of what film-makers call a
'cut', he may offend against the laws of scholarly dramaturgy,
but in doing so he proves himself capable of the same
aesthetic boldness which shows 'before' and 'after' in a single
pictorial continuum, just as his scandalous sympathy with the
hated Persians sets a precedent for the kind of imaginative
leap into the other person's skin and psyche without which
dramatic dialogue, in the largest sense, would lack the
tension we associate with theatre. The elastic anatomy of

dramatic time is one of Aeschylus' greatest (and most unsung) discoveries.

Persians is sophisticated in its simplicities, ambiguous in its 'propagandistic' patriotism, deceptive in its apparently smooth progression. In declaring, however sympathetically, the ruinous consequences of absolute monarchy, it is, by implication, an advertisement for democracy, and hence for the kind of dialogue from which the Persian elders explicitly excuse themselves: that of equals speaking to their rulers as equals. *Persians* is on one note only to those with monotonous minds; it is 'unsatisfactory' only to scholars who, with their enviable ability to detect needles, sometimes fail to notice the haystacks.

Seven Against Thebes

The Theban myth-cycle begins with the foundation of the city by Cadmus, and ends, seven generations later, with the city's capture by sons of the seven champions of Aeschylus' play. The group of myths favoured by dramatists centres on Cadmus' great-grandson Laius and his children and grand-children. Brought up in exile, Laius outraged the gods by a homosexual liaison with Chrysippus, prince of Pisa. He fled for his life to Thebes, where he married Queen Jocasta and took the throne. Apollo foretold that he would have a son, who would kill his father and murder his mother. To prevent this, Laius exposed the newborn child on Mount Cithaeron.

The events which followed are known to modern audiences chiefly from Sophocles' *King Oedipus*: the rescuing of the child Oedipus, his visit to the Delphic oracle, his murder of Laius, his encounter with the Sphinx, his marriage to Jocasta, and the punishment he inflicted on himself when he discovered the truth. As the myth (though not Sophocles) continues, he lived on afterwards in Thebes, until his sons Eteocles and Polynices served him a slave's portion of food instead of the royal prerogative. He cursed them, saying that iron would divide their inheritance, and they would go to the Underworld on the same day, killed by one another. He then went into exile, led by his daughter Antigone, and some time later died.

Eteocles and Polynices both claimed the throne of Thebes. When Eteocles won, Polynices asked King Adrastus of Argos to raise an army and support his claim. Seven champions led the Argive army: Adrastus, Polynices, Tydeus, Capaneus, Hippomedon, Amphiaraus and Parthenopaeus. They attacked Thebes, each leading his men against one of the city's seven gates, where he was challenged by a Theban champion. At the seventh gate, Eteocles and Polynices met in single combat, and each killed the other. Once again, the events which followed – King Creon's order that the defenders should be buried with honour but the attackers left to rot; Antigone's defiance and death – are well known from Sophocles. The myth-cycle ends by telling how these events outraged all Greece, how Theseus attacked the city, executed Creon and buried the dead, and how a second group of champions, sons of the original seven, besieged the city but found it empty: all the inhabitants, warned by Tiresias (who all through these events had given infallible prophecies) that the gods would no longer protect them, had fled.

In 467BC Aeschylus won first prize with a quartet of plays on this cycle: the tragedies *Laius*, *Oedipus* and *Seven Against Thebes* and the satyr-play *Sphinx*. Only *Seven Against Thebes* survives. Though little is known about the missing plays, it seems reasonable that their titles suggest their contents, and that the tragedies formed a trilogy. *Seven Against Thebes* is therefore even more of a torso than *Suppliants* or *Prometheus Bound* (both of which came first, not last, in groups of plays). Its difficulties, for scholars, are compounded by the fact that a new ending appears to have been added some time after 467, introducing the characters of Antigone and Ismene (whose story is not otherwise mentioned) and probably not by Aeschylus. Textual problems have earned the play a reputation as both unsatisfactory and difficult.

As we read *Seven Against Thebes*, however, or see it in the theatre, such criticisms fade away. The play is an all-engulfing torrent of language (almost certainly paralleled in the original production by music and dance). It is, so to speak, in three 'movements', the Chorus-led laments of the first and last thirds framing the actor-led pomp and martial ceremony of the central description of the champions. Some writers scorn the idea that Greek tragedy in performance might be more like modern oratorio or cantata. If it is an inadequate way to 'realise' most surviving plays onstage, *Seven Against Thebes* is the exception. There is no action at all apart from half a dozen inessential exits and entrances. There is no philosophical discussion: the issues are straightforward and are presented head-on, especially by Eteocles. There is no forward movement: Aeschylus neither leads up to the deaths of Eteocles and Polynices, making them a climax, nor falls back from them afterwards (as he does, for example, with the death of Clytemnestra in *Libation-Bearers* or the acquittal of Orestes in *Eumenides*). The deaths take their place in a sequence of events which are, dramatically speaking, as static and unvaried as tableaux in a tapestry or the movements of a symphony.

Comparisons with music go further than mere form. Each of the play's three sections is a sequence of statements and responses, the response in each case 'closing' and 'confirming' the thought broached in the statement. (This is akin to the 'open/close' structure of many themes in classical music, for example those of Mozart or early Beethoven.) There is constant repetition of ideas, either by complete statement or in fragmentary allusion. Longer speeches, or passages in new metres, punctuate the flow, shifting the direction or pace of thought. The central section is more static, less varied, than the 'movements' on either side. (In modern productions, with a female Chorus, the outer and central sections even offer different voice-timbres; one wonders if this was paralelled – and if so, how – in the original, all male, Greek production.) Most striking of all, the 'thematic' construction of the play does not depend only on such large matters as the contrast between the Chorus' panic and Eteocles' impatience at the beginning, or between the Soldier's description of each of the seven champions and Eteocles' measured but no less high-flown response. Woven into the texture, like the small details of harmony or scoring which give life to a musical score, are fragmented, allusive, many-times-repeated flickers of ideas. The curse on the house of Laius and the Fury which oversees it; Eteocles' (unexplained, unexamined) disgust for the female sex (echoing the family curse); the sounds of war –

none of these are described or debated at length (as the curse on the house of Atreus is in the *Oresteia*, or the arrogance of power is in *Prometheus Bound*); instead they are slipped regularly into our minds, often by single words or phrases, colouring the main themes and utterances of the play.

Cerebral analysis of this kind is perhaps more likely to occur to readers of the text than to spectators in the theatre. As one watches the play, however, one is unlikely to miss overall changes of mood and tempo, patterns of statement and response, and the many incidental effects, both large (for example the grand, relaxed 'settling in' to such passages as that beginning 'Gods of Thebes, come, come gods of this land', 109ff) and small (the 'night sky' on Tydeus' shield, 389ff; the muzzle-pipes, 467; the dead stop after 'Polynices, your own brother', 632; the 'flags of doom' in 958, turning in on itself the prancing battle-imagery from earlier in the play). Aeschylus' poetry in this play matches his best surviving work: the early choruses of *Agamemnon*, say, or Prometheus' description of Io's wanderings, or the Egyptian scene in *Suppliants*. All such excellence would be immediately apparent to an audience – indeed, more obvious in performance than to someone merely reading the text. And Aeschylus, showman as well as poet, added another ingredient, whose effect is lost today but must have electrified his contemporaries. In 467, when *Seven Against Thebes* was performed, memories of the Persian invasion of 13 years before, of the devastation wrought by war, would still be raw, both adding poignancy to the choral laments of the play and pointing up the militaristic bombast of the Soldier's descriptions of the seven champions. Aeschylus flaunted no victory at Salamis here (as he did in *Persians*), offered no praise, overt or covert, for Athens' gods, leaders or fighting men. An artist chooses what best fits each occasion – and the resonances Aeschylus provided in this play were not only appropriate to the end of his treatment of the doomed house of Laius, the dying fall of Thebes, but must have had an unexpected political relevance – no less pungent for being unstated – at the time.

Suppliants

In myth, Danaus and Aegyptus were twin sons of Baal (Belos) and Anchinoe, daughter of the river Nile. Aegyptus ruled Arabia and Egypt, and Danaus ruled Libya. Each brother had fifty children, Aegyptus sons and Danaus daughters (the 'Danaids'), and Aegyptus suggested a dynastic marriage between them. But Danaus, warned by the gods that Aegyptus was really planning to murder him and all his family, escaped with his daughters to Greece. They landed in the Peloponnese, in the swampy estuary of the river Lerna (where Heracles later killed the Hydra), and made their way to Argos.

Having given the Danaids shelter, the people of Argos were besieged by an Egyptian army led by Aegyptus' sons. Danaus ended the siege by agreeing to the marriage – but gave each of his daughters a dagger to hide in her hair on the wedding night. Each daughter stabbed her husband dead except for Hypermnestra, who pitied, loved and spared Lynceus. She was tried before the people for disobedience, and Aphrodite spoke up for her, winning her freedom. The other Danaids lived the rest of their mortal lives happily, but after death were punished for the murders by being forced to bail a lake with sieves.

Suppliants is the only surviving play of what was probably a tetralogy based on this myth: three linked tragedies followed by a satyr play about the Danaid Amymone, rescued by Poseidon from a satyr who was trying to rape her. *Suppliants*, dealing with the Danaids' arrival and acceptance at Argos, seems to set the scene and establish the background and themes of a larger drama, in a similar way to the first half of *Agamemnon*. If the rest of the trilogy was patterned like the *Oresteia* (the only surviving trilogy we have to go on), it is possible to imagine what the later plays might have contained. *Sons of Aegyptus* could have been set during the siege of Argos, perhaps ending with the mass marriage; *Danaids* could have dealt with Hypermnestra's trial and the resolution of the moral issues. But there is no firm evidence for this or any other division. Indeed, *Suppliants* makes perfect sense as a single, free-standing play, and some scholars dispute the existence of a trilogy at all.

The simple form of the play – chiefly choral song, and dialogues between one or two actors and the Chorus Leader – led people to believe for years that it was early, from what scholars loftily called the 'primitive' stage of Greek tragedy. One argument in support of this theory was that there were 50 Danaids in the myth, and there were supposed to be 50 Chorus-members in early 5th-century drama (as compared with the 15 of later in the century). But in 1952 a papyrus was discovered linking *Suppliants* with *Sons of Aegyptus* and *Danaids*, and suggesting that the trilogy was performed at the height of Aeschylus' career, probably in 463BC in a competition in which he took first prize and Sophocles came second. This find caused confusion in the minds of those who found the play 'primitive'. Their best explanation was that it must have been a hitherto-unperformed early work, taken out of the cupboard (and possibly elaborated and given companion-pieces) for the 460s performance.

This sort of quibbling seems not just unimportant, but also nonsense. In the first place, if a dramatist of Aeschylus' stature *had* resuscitated early work, it is unlikely that he would have left it as 'primitive' as the play's detractors claim. In the second place, there is nothing at all second-rate about the play. The notion of primitiveness depends on a preconceived view of what Greek tragedies ought to be like – a view which few surviving examples (none by Aeschylus) can be said to support. If it is obligatory to comment on *Suppliants*' quality by comparing it with something else, it less recalls the putative chorus-and-actor work of Thespis and other early playwrights than Aeschylus' own *Agamemnon*. For power of language, for imagery, density of thought and theatrical energy, it stands with his finest work.

Two examples, from dozens, can be chosen to make the point. First is the surefooted characterisation-through-dialogue of both Danaus and the Argive king. When we watch plays by Sophocles and Euripides, interest is more often in progressive revelation than in development of both situation and character. This is so even in plays dominated by such powerful creations as Electra, Hecuba, Medea or

Philoctetes. Gradual unmasking of a pre-determined state of things, as mysterious to the characters in the action as it is to the spectators, allows Sophocles and Euripides to explore every possibility for irony and for the reinforcement of expectation. That exploration creates the feeling of theatrical danger which is such a marked feature of their plays. In Aeschylus, by contrast, danger comes from open-endedness. Characters and situations are not stable, to be unpeeled for us like onions. They are ambiguous and unpredictable. Every line, instead of deliciously or terrifyingly confirming what we know or suspect, raises questions, distracts us from complacency, makes us think. In this process, characterisation is just one item among many: it is balanced, for example, by the philosophical suggestiveness and plurality of the choral utterances. But, in *Suppliants*, both Danaus and the Argive king are unpredictable, changing people. We could never guess, from Danaus' Polonius-like early speeches, the iron-willed regality of his final appearance, which both grows out of the situation and may lay the groundwork for future action (without the rest of the trilogy we cannot be sure). Apprehension, open-heartedness, decisiveness and caution flicker through every speech by the Argive king, changing almost line by line and phrase by phrase.

The second example of excellence is the Egyptian scene. This is a theatrical 'turn', a bravura sequence similar to the Cassandra scene in *Agamemnon* – and like that scene, it derives its energy and fascination from Aeschylus' use of language. He plays with sound and syntax (see note 31, page 149) like someone composing music rather than words. Two things in particular keep us on the edge of expectation: the way in which the overarching form of the scene allows pointful contrast between the Egyptian's move from fragmented incoherence to silkiness and the unvarying panic and distraction of the Chorus, and the way in which the Argive king's entrance sends the dialogue spiralling in a new and unexpected direction – a surprise analogous to the appearance of a new theme in a piece of music. Throughout the scene, Aeschylus continually invites the audience to second-guess its progress, and then trumps those guesses. He plays games with us, in a way possible only in the performing arts. If going to see his plays was a spectacularly satisfying occupation, scenes like this, rather than flying Choruses or simulated earthquakes, were what made it so.

It might be thought that excellences of this kind must escape modern spectators, that the gulfs of time and language between us and Aeschylus must be unbridgable. To an extent that is undeniable. But paradoxically, even in translation, we can appreciate the theatrical energy of the Egyptian scene or the subtlety with which the characterisation of Danaus or the Argive king matches the open-ended nature and 'meaning' of the action, far more easily than some of the more obvious-seeming elements (choral dancing, say) which must have made this play 'work' for Athenian spectators. Our major difficulty is imagining what the stage picture must have been like for them. It is impossible to answer even the simplest question: how many people were onstage at any given time? The dialogue talks of 50 Danaids, each with a maidservant, and of soldiers in chariots accompanying the Argive king; some editors suggest, further, that the Egyptian was accompanied by sailors – one scholar even imagined all 50 sons of Aegyptus pounding after him – and that a second Chorus, of Argive women, led the Danaids out in procession at the end of the play. At the austere end of the same spectrum, the play can be staged with two actors and a Chorus of minimal size, less even than the 12-15 of 5th-century Athenian productions. As to what these performers, few or many, did, we have no evidence at all. The play has little dramatic action; 'action' is in the language and in the thought behind it. But that is no more a drawback than in any other Aeschylus play. Even without music and dance, *Suppliants* passes two of the main tests of 'greatness' in drama. It simultaneously opens our minds and fills them, it makes us think even as it satisfies us – and it does so in ways which are perfectly apparent on the page (just as well, as it might otherwise not have survived) but which double and redouble their effect, simply and thrillingly, when it is given its proper medium: performance.

Prometheus Bound

In the Greek cycle of creation-myths, the Olympian gods were descended from earlier powers: Titans, the offspring of Earth and Sky. The gods, led by Zeus, dethroned the Titans and there was war in heaven. Prometheus advised his fellow-Titans to use brain rather than brawn – and when they ignored him, he transferred his loyalty and his cunning to Zeus. The gods won; the Titans were exiled or imprisoned, and Zeus rewarded his supporters. However, he quarrelled with Prometheus over human beings. Prometheus had created them from mud, and was eager to give them intelligence, the gods' prerogative. But Zeus, fearful that they might also demand equal power, wanted them destroyed. Prometheus stole a spark of Hephaestus' sacred fire, the source of all knowledge, and gave it to mortals. For this Zeus chained him to a rock in the deserts of Scythia, in the hinterland between Earth (being) and Chaos (non-being). Each day a monster was sent to feed on his liver, which was miraculously renewed each night. Two conditions had to be met before Prometheus could be released: he must reveal a secret which he alone knew and which threatened Zeus' power, and another god must agree to surrender immortality and take his place.

Prometheus hung in torment (or, in some versions, lay plunged on his rock in the depths of the Underworld) for an age of the world, at the end of which Zeus pardoned the Titans and ended their exile. This prompted Prometheus, too, to relent. He revealed the secret (that if Zeus impregnated Thetis she would bear a son greater than his father). An immortal agreed to take Prometheus' place: Chiron the centaur, in agony after being accidentally wounded by one of Heracles' poisoned arrows. Heracles killed the liver-devouring monster and set Prometheus free.

Aeschylus wrote several plays based on these myths. The best known in his own lifetime was *Prometheus Freed*, now lost. It was written at the end of his life, at about the same time as the *Oresteia*, and its action (Prometheus is persuaded, by Mother Earth and the Chorus of Titans, to bow to Zeus' authority and accept a place of honour in the new world-order) may have echoed the themes of reconciliation and harmony which close *Eumenides*. Scholars disagree about how *Prometheus Bound* relates to it. Some say that the plays formed a linked pair, complete in themselves; others that they made a trilogy with a third (lost) play, *Prometheus Firebringer*; others that each was self-contained. There is, indeed, continuing debate about the actual authenticity of *Prometheus Bound*. Opinion ranges from one extreme (that it is one hundred percent Aeschylus, one of his noblest works) to the other (that it was cobbled together by others, perhaps from an Aeschylean draft, either as a companion-piece to *Prometheus Freed* or for some provincial performance, perhaps in Sicily: see note 38, page 151).

The authenticity arguments are hardly fascinating for what they reveal of the scholarly mind: one might ask who cares who wrote any given play, so long as it is a satisfying work of art. Their interest is in what they show of Aeschylus' style and working method, and of the qualities we admire in him. Four main subjects of controversy are spectacle, quality of verse, thought and the Io scene. Briefly put, those who argue against Aeschylus' authorship say that the spectacle – the nailing of Prometheus to the rock, the flying entries of Ocean and the Chorus, and the final thunderstorm and earthquake – is dramatically inept, a series of stage-effects not justified by or integrated with the action (as, for example, Agamemnon's entry into his palace in *Agamemnon* or the Ghost scene in *Eumenides* are integrated). They object that the verse varies wildly in quality, and that at its worst (for example the opening scene or the dialogue in which Prometheus is persuaded to recount Io's wanderings) it is wooden and repetitive. They claim that the thought, similarly, veers from the sublimity of Prometheus' soliloquies to the scrappiness and bathos of much of what the Chorus says. And finally, they complain that the Io scene is irrelevant, a self-contained insert which the author has made little effort to link with the theme of the whole play or with the action on either side of it.

Those who support Aeschylus' authorship have plausible answers to each of these 'objections'. They say that problems about spectacle vanish as soon as we assume that it was described only, not represented onstage. They suggest that the play is more a stage-poem, a kind of dramatic cantata, than a piece of busy narrative action, and that its static nature dictates, and is brilliantly served by, the ebb and flow of the verse. They claim that the movement between linguistic limpidity and complexity, so far from being inept, is carefully organised, and that the elevation of Prometheus' thought and utterance is enhanced by its plainer surroundings, not least by the Choral passages (which are deliberately shorter and less ornate than in Aeschylus' other surviving plays). Finally, they say that the Io scene is not an ill-sewn insert but a *coup de théâtre*, at once a deliberate jolt to our thinking about the nature of Zeus and a stunning stage effect, in which Io's restless dancing and edgy verse (perhaps complementing similarly energetic Choral dancing) are contrasted with Prometheus' granitic stillness. In short, Aeschylus' defenders claim that, as in all his surviving work, form in *Prometheus Bound* precisely serves meaning, that the play progresses by lyrical contrasts of music and movement rather than in linear dramatic flow.

A final strand in the authenticity argument is hard to discuss in the absence of more than fragments of *Prometheus Freed*. It is the issue of what we are shown in the play(s) of Zeus' nature and purposes. In *Prometheus Bound* Zeus is presented exclusively through the eyes of Prometheus, his bitter enemy: even Hermes' choice of service to his Olympian master is glossed in terms as unflattering to both parties as possible. Our limited knowledge of *Prometheus Freed* suggests that in that play, by contrast, Zeus' wise and forgiving side was stressed. The dramatic diptych moved from philosophical dissonance to harmony, and the uncompromisingly harsh world-view in *Prometheus Bound* was essential to make that movement possible.

Because this reconstruction of the diptych depends not on evidence but on the assumption that the end of *Prometheus Freed* was similar to that of *Eumenides*, some writers have dismissed the whole idea of linkage between the plays – a decision which leaves the tyrant-Zeus of *Prometheus Bound* in what may nowadays seem somewhat melodramatic highlighting. Indeed, this reading of his character partly accounts for the play's enormous popularity in 19th-century Europe (where it outranked all Aeschylus' other surviving works). To such writers as Goethe, Shelley and Hugo, and to their fervent readers and admirers, Prometheus seemed the emblem of heroic, romantic struggle against despotism, a freedom-fighter to stand beside such other legendary and literary heroes as Egmont or William Tell. If he was to seem all-noble, it helped that his adversary Zeus was all-wicked; and suggestions that Prometheus' own behaviour and attitudes were questionable, or that the play's picture of Zeus chimed with nothing either in other surviving Greek tragedies or in ancient philosophical and religious attitudes, were simply never made.

The ideas (first) that the play we have is no more than a magnificent ruin, like the pillars and lintels of some imposing temple, and (second) that reconstruction of its original context – whether diptych, triptych or a group of unrelated plays performed on the same day in the theatre – might completely change our view of it, are recent, and have caused as much alarm as interest. Hence, perhaps, the upsurge in authenticity arguments: it is easier to condemn an 'awkward' work of art as spurious than to come to critical terms with what it meant, and means. But this latter approach may in fact be more profitable. It starts from the premises (on the evidence, at least as supportable as any others) that Aeschylus wrote most of *Prometheus Bound* as we have it here, and that he not only knew exactly what he was trying to do, but had the theatrical means to do it, including the music and dance, so crucial to the effect, which we have no way of reconstructing. The fact that modern readers and audiences find so many strangenesses in the play is not proof that it is a 'lesser' work, but rather that we still have work to do – enthralling, rewarding work – to understand.

(*Note: The line-numbering alongside the texts relates to the Greek original rather than to the original translation. The superior numbers in the texts refer to the Notes at the end of the book.*)

PERSIANS

Characters

QUEEN ATOSSA
MESSENGER
GHOST OF DARIUS
XERXES
CHORUS OF OLD MEN OF SUSA
ATTENDANTS (silent parts)

Before Darius' tomb, outside the palace doors of Susa.
Enter CHORUS.

CHORUS.
   You see trust. They trusted us,
   The Persians who marched on Greece.
   Seniority's office, our task
   Imposed by Xerxes,
   Darius' son: keep safe
   The royal gold, this seat of kings.
   Oh, when will our lord return?
   That swarm of men, gold-glittering?
   Drums of ill-omen beat,
   Beat in our hearts.   10
   Now Asia's might's afield,
   Our hearts all ache for him,
   Majesty.
   Why no message, no herald
   Galloping, galloping?

   From Susa's towers they swarmed,
   From Agbatana, from ancient Cissia:
   On foot, on horse, by ship,
   Brigades, battalions,
   Thronging for war.   20
   Their lords' names:
   Amistres, Artaphrenes,
   Megabates, Astaspes,
   Marshals of Persia,
   Kings loyal to one great king,
   Of one great force the pride.
   Master-bowmen, spearsmen, cavaliers:
   Fearful to see, more fearful far
   To fight: to dare their sole resolve.
   Artembares, chariot-lord,
   Masistres, Imaeus arrow-straight,   30
   Sosthanes horse-master,
   Pharandaces.
   More men wide Nile sends forth,
   Swirling, mother of mortals:
   Susiscanes, Pegastagon Aegyptus' son,
   Arsames, priest-prince of Memphis,

Ariomardus who holds mysterious Thebes in fee.
Marsh-Arabs, crafty oarsmen,
40   A host past numbering.
Soft Lydians; Ionians
Who fringe our continent,
Their generals Metrogathes,
Arcteus the Brave, kings in their pride.
From Sardis next:
Chariots thronging, a stream of gold,
Like javelins, three-horsed, four-horsed,
Terror to behold.
Next, sacred Tmolus' regiment,
50   All set to hoop Greeks for slaves:
Mardon, Tharybis, anvils of iron,
Mysian spearsmen. See! Golden Babylon
Mints sailors, a shoal, mints archers,
Their trust their bending bows.
All Asia's blades are drawn:
Crowding, thronging to answer
Their king's dread call to arms.
60   The flower of the Persian land is gone.
Their motherland,
Asia who mothered them,
Waits for them, weeps for them;
Families, wives,
Stretch fearful days upon the rack of time.

The crossing's made. The king's machine,
The city-smashing host, makes bridgehead
On alien shore. Now Helle's gulf
70   Stands cable-stitched, sea's neck
Bridged tight, road-yoked[1].

Lord Xerxes, teeming Asia's master,
Now view-halloos his pack against the land.
Stern generals, sure on sea, on land,
His confidence. Now, living gold[2],
80   He dazzles like the gods.
Dragon-eyes, iron looks,
A shoal of hands, of sails;
From hurtling chariot

He fires at spear-famed Greeks
Ares the war god,
Arrowing the foe.

A flood of men, a cataract!
Who'll face it down?
What weapons, what battle-cries
Can dam this sea?   90
Persia's army – Persians! –
Unstoppable.

Heaven's tricks and snares –
What mortal ever cheats them?
Quickfoot, high-leaping,
Who slips the cull?
Fate beckons, smiles,
Seduces:
You're trapped, you die.   100

God-sent, of old,
Our destiny since time began:
Tower-toppling war,
Hard-galloping,
City-sacking.

New knowledge now:
They scan the sea,
Wind-lathered, sacrosanct;   110
They tame it, bind it,
Swarm across.

Our hearts black-cloaked,
Fear-torn. O-ah!
Fear for Persia's marching might,
Fear for Susa
Widowed, stripped, unmanned.

From Cissia's proud citadel   120
Grief-cries, o-ah!,
Shrieks of women echoing,
Beat breasts,
Claw finery to rags.

Our army – knights, foot-soldiers –
Swarms from the hive,
130 Yokes continents,
Makes two lands one
And swarms across.

Empty marriage-beds, filled with tears.
All painful smiles,
They flung their men, like keen,
Hot spears, to war,
Themselves to widowhood.

CHORUS LEADER.
140 Come, Persians,
Here in this ancient place
Sit down, discuss, debate.
How fares lord Xerxes,
Son of Darius, king of kings?
Have our bowmen triumphed?
Have lance-thrusts, spear-casts
Given Greece the prize?

Enter QUEEN, *attended*.

150 Look: like a god she comes,
Light to our eyes,
The Queen, his majesty's royal mother.
I bow.
In humble courtesy,
As is the law, I speak to her.

Majesty, of deep-gowned Persian womanhood the
pearl,
Mother of Xerxes, our respects, Darius' worthy wife
Who shared the bed of Persia's god, and to a god gave
birth,
Unless the luck has changed, for all our Persian host.

QUEEN.
Why else should I leave those gilded halls
160 Where Darius and I lay down, and come to you?
Care claws my heart. Thoughts haunt me. Friends,

I share with you secret fears. Is all our wealth
Now tramped to dust, our glory scattered
That Darius, with God's good help, raised up?
Two-pronged the thought unspoken in my heart:
What point in royal pomp if men be gone? What light
For manly muscle shines, unfed by power?
We're rich – look round! – but where's our guiding light?
A house is blind unless its lord is there.
Thus stands our case. Be then my counsellors: 170
Your age, your wisdom. Sirs, in this our state
I choose, and ground my trust in you.

CHORUS LEADER.
Majesty, queen of all Persia, ask no more:
You own the loyalty which now you ask.
In word and deed our energies are yours.

QUEEN.
Dreams haunt me.
Night after night they come,
Since my son drummed up his army,
Marched on Greece. Dream after dream –
And none so clear as in this last night.   180
Two women came: well-dressed,
One in Persian elegance, one Dorian.
In bearing both belittled us today:
In beauty flawless sisters;
In race identical. Their native lands?
One Greek, one … not-Greek.³
Suddenly they quarrelled, the pair of them.
My son separated them, calmed them,
Tried to yoke them to his chariot.   190
One stood quiet, obedient,
Proud in her harness. The other
Bucked, tore free the bridle, plunged
Out of control, and smashed the yoke.
My son stumbled. Darius came,
His father, and wept for him. When Xerxes saw,
He ripped his own clothes to rags.

200   That was the dream. When morning came,
In running water I washed away the omen,
Ran to the altar, carrying in my hand –
This hand, the hand ordained –
Gifts to the gods to take all ill away.
Instead, an eagle, fluttering in fear,
Settled on Phoebus' holy hearth.
I watched. Mute with fear.
A hawk next. Swooped, perched – the talons! –
Raking, clawing its rival's head. Down, down,
The eagle cowered. Offered itself. No fight.

210   I saw this terror, saw as I tell you now.
Know this:
My son, successful, will dazzle every eye.
But if he fails, he'll not step down:
Long as he lives, this land is his.

CHORUS LEADER.
We answer, Mother. No fright in what we say,
And no false cheer. The gods, Majesty, the gods now
    need
Your supplication. Omens of evil in what you saw –
May the gods discard them, make them drop unripe.
May blessings rain on you, your son, your state,
Your friends. And next, libations pour

220   To Earth and the Dead below. In deference
Beg Darius your consort, whom you saw last night,
To send good things from Dark below to Light above
For you, for Xerxes, and snatch all evil down
To lie entombed. Pious advice! We offer it
In hope, in trust, that all may yet be well.

QUEEN.
My lord, your words, your reading of my dream
Show loyalty – to Xerxes, to the royal house.
God send it so! As you suggest, good prayers
To Heaven above, to those below who wish us well,
I'll offer up, inside. For now, one question more:

230   My lords, this … Athens. Where on Earth – ?

CHORUS LEADER.
Far, lady. Where sets our lord the Sun.

QUEEN.
One town. Why should Xerxes want it so?

CHORUS LEADER.
If Athens falls, all Greece submits.

QUEEN.
Have they such soldiers?

CHORUS LEADER.
You know them, lady. They hurt the Medes before.[4]

QUEEN.
What are they, archers, who bend the well-sprung bow?

CHORUS LEADER.
No! Spearsmen, hand-to-hand; their armour, shields.

QUEEN.
They're wealthy – ?

CHORUS LEADER.
They've silver, lady, springing from the earth.[5]   240

QUEEN.
Who shepherds them? Their warlord – who?

CHORUS LEADER.
Call them no mortal's slaves. They bow to none.

QUEEN.
They nerve themselves to face the foe?

CHORUS LEADER.
They crushed Darius' heroes.

QUEEN.
Cold words for parents of our marching men!

CHORUS LEADER.
You'll know soon, Majesty. Clear words.
A soldier, look, running to bring us news.
Good words or bad, he'll tell them straight.

Enter MESSENGER.

MESSENGER.
Cities of Asia,

250   Land of Persia, fortune's anchorage,
    At a single stroke our good luck's gone,
    Our flower of glory withered.
    O cruel to bring first cruel news!
    I must, I must. Persians,
    The whole barbarian force is lost.

CHORUS.
    Pain stabs,
    Stabs sudden pain.
    Persians, hear and weep.

MESSENGER.
260   Our whole expedition wrecked.
    I never thought to see home again.

CHORUS.
    We've lived
    Too long, if these old ears
    Must hear such pain.

MESSENGER.
    I saw it all. No hearsay. Persians,
    I tell what these eyes saw.

CHORUS.
    O-toto-to-ee!
    In vain they marched,
270   That forest of weapons,
    From Asia to Greece, to death.

MESSENGER.
    Stiff corpses choke Salamis' sands,
    The dunes beyond.

CHORUS.
    O-toto-to-ee!
    Loved ones, bloated,
    Battle-cloaks their shrouds,
    Bobbing, bobbing on the sea.

MESSENGER.
    Their bows: useless. A whole army, crushed
    As ship impacted ship.

CHORUS.
    Shrill voices, weep.   280
    Persians, cry.
    Gods heap disaster,
    Waste our men.

MESSENGER.
    Salamis, vilest of names!
    Athens! To say it is to weep.

CHORUS.
    Athens! Death to her enemies.
    Women of Persia,
    Husbandless, childless,
    We weep for you.

QUEEN.
    Blow on blow. I said nothing: 290
    What words can equal this?
    Yet when gods send pain,
    What can mortals do but bear it?
    Speak calmly. The whole disaster –
    Groan if you must, but tell it plain.
    Are any ... not dead? The princes,
    The high command? Are there ... gaps
    Among the leaders of the people?

MESSENGER.
    Lord Xerxes lives and sees the light.

QUEEN.
    Your words are dawn to this my house.   300
    Bright daylight shines from darkness.

MESSENGER.
    Artembares, who reined ten thousand horse,
    Rolls on the tideline at Salamis.
    Dadaces the chiliarch, speared
    Mid-jump from ship to shore;
    Lord Tenagon of Bactria
    Snags on sea-scourged rocks.

Arsames, Lilaeus, Argastes,
Below the cliff where rock-doves nest,
310 Swirl and butt, swirl and butt.
Allies from Egypt: Pharnuchus,
Arcteus, Adeues, Pheresseues,
All from one ship, all dead.
Matallus of Chrysa, myriarch:
Death scabs his black beard red.
Dead Magian Arabus; dead Bactrian Artabes,
Horse-lord, ruled thirty thousand men,
Now rules one narrow grave.
320 Amistris; Amphistreus, spearsman of death;
Brave Ariomardus, Sardis' woe; Seisames the
       Mysian;
Tharybis from Lyrna, handsome,
Who five times fifty ships deployed,
Death-wasted lies, his beauty spoiled;
Gallant Syennesis, Cilician king,
Swamped by enemies, dealt death and died.
So many leaders! So many names!
330 Disasters teemed for us; I name but few.

QUEEN.
Ai-ee! I scale the peak of pain.
Howl, shriek for Persia. Shame!
Begin again. These Greeks –
What swarm of ships had they,
To risk, to dare attack
Our Persian armada? Head-on? How dared they?

MESSENGER.
If numbers were all, we'd ride in triumph now.
For the Greeks: some ten times thirty sail,
340 With ten besides, crack warships.
For Xerxes: main fleet one thousand,
Fast galleons, two hundred and seven more.
The numbers are exact. We hardly failed
In numbers. Some power from the gods bore down;
Tipped scales; Fate cheated.
The gods it was kept Athens, Athene's city, safe.

QUEEN.
The city stands?

MESSENGER.
Its soldiers live. It stands.

QUEEN.
Tell how it began, the ships, their clash.   350
Who were first in line: the Greeks? –
My son, pluming himself on that great fleet?

MESSENGER.
Some demon, Majesty, some spite began disaster.
A man came to your son – a Greek, an Athenian.
Greek nerve would never hold, he said.
As soon as darkness fell, they'd leap on board,
Grab oars and row for their lives
In all directions. Xerxes believed him.   360
Why should he suspect the hand of God?
He sent word to all his captains. 'As soon
As the Sun withdraws his shafts that light the Earth,
As soon as darkness tenants the evening sky,
Action stations! Divide the fleet in three.
One group row round the island. The rest
Block access to open water. If any Greeks slip past,
If they trick any ships to freedom,   370
Your heads shall pay for it.' Proud orders:
How could he know what future gods had planned?
Our men, obedient, well-trained, ate dinner,
Then each sailor looped and tied his oar in place.
As soon as the Sun's bright light declined
And night crept in, each master-oarsman,
Each man-at-arms, embarked. The longships sailed.
Calling out to one another, they rowed
In line ahead across the strait. As ordered,   380
The captains kept them rowing to and fro
All night. All night –
And not one glimpse of Greeks!
Day dawned. White horses streaked the sky.
Light dazzled – and a huge Greek shout,
Crashing, echoing. We cowered: 390
Our plan had made us clowns.

These were no runaways, shrieking for safety;
These were fighters, nerving themselves for war.
The trumpet flamed and fired their ranks.
Their oars flayed sea to foam. Fast, fast they came,
Parading for battle: the right wing first,

400   The rest in good order. And all the time,
From every throat, we heard their battle-cry:
'On, sons of Greece! Set free
Your fatherland, your children, wives,
Homes of your ancestors and temples of your gods!
Save all, or all is lost!'[6]
On our side a roar, a tide of answering cries.
The fight began. Ship pounced on ship.
Bronze beaks stripped wood. First blood to Greece:
An Athenian warship rammed its prey,

410   A galleon from Tyre, sheared all its poop away[7].
Now, full ahead, ship skewered ship. At first
Our Persian fleet held firm. But soon
Ships choked the straits; no room to turn, to help.
Oars smashed; sterns caved in;
The bronze beaks bit and bit.
The Greeks snatched their advantage,
Surrounding us, pounding us.
Ship after ship capsized;

420   The sea was swamped with wreckage, corpses,
The beaches, dunes, all piggy-backed with dead.
Our ships broke ranks, tried one by one
To slip the line. The Greeks, like fishermen
With a haul of tunny netted and trapped,
Stabbed, gaffed with snapped-off oars
And broken spars, smashed, smashed, till all the sea
Was one vast salty soup of shrieks and cries.
At last black night came down and hid the scene.

430   Disaster on disaster. I could take ten days,
And not tell all. Be sure of this: never before
Have so many thousands died on a single day.

QUEEN.
Aiee! Destruction, wave on wave,
Breaks on us, our people drowned.

MESSENGER.
> My news is scarce half told.
> Ruin treads on ruin,
> Sorrow beyond all bearing.

QUEEN.
> What can you add,
> What misery,
> To tip the scale of grief?   440

MESSENGER.
> Princes of Persia, who gave brave nature point,
> The best in spirit and in blood the best,
> In loyalty the King's own paragons,[8]
> Are dead. Ignobly, like common men.

QUEEN.
> Lords! I tremble.
> Speak, sir. Tell how they died.

MESSENGER.
> There is an island, facing Salamis:
> Small, too tight for ships.
> On its rocky shore, God dances: Pan.
> There Xerxes sent lords, picked men.   450
> The enemy fleet gone down, he said,
> Greeks would scramble there for safety.
> Easy victims. Our enemies would die,
> Our friends would live. He said.
> But when the gods gave Greece the fight,
> They noosed the place with warships,
> A ring of bronze. Where could we turn?
> Stones, arrows from springing bows,   460
> Destruction. They streamed ashore,
> Yelling, butchering. Life died.
> No survivors. On the mainland,
> Throned on a high headland,
> Xerxes peered down on the killing-ground,
> Saw everything. He tore his clothes; he groaned,
> Sent word to his army: 'Break ranks and run'.
> Disaster on disaster. Majesty, weep now.   470

QUEEN.
> What demon spite cheats Persia's plans?
> A bitter reckoning: brave Athens owed,
> My Xerxes paid. Were they not enough,
> The Persians who died at Marathon?
> Lord Xerxes went to balance that account –
> And paid, and paid.
> Tell me: clearly, leave nothing out.
> Some ships escaped? You left them – where?

MESSENGER.
480
> Some ships survived. Their captains
> Scrambled before the wind. No order.
> The army, what was left of it,
> Died on Boeotian soil, thirst-parched,
> Gasping. A few of us reached Phocis,
> Doris, the Melian gulf,
> Rich farmland watered by sweet Spercheius;
> The Achaean plain; the towns of Thessaly –
> We were starving, they took us in;
490
> Still many died, too weak to eat or drink.
> We struggled on: Magnesia; Macedonia;
> Across the Axius; the marshes of Bolbe;
> To Edonian territory, high Pangaeus.
> That night, the gods sent frost, frost in autumn.
> The river froze; soldiers who'd never prayed before
> Fell on their knees, kissed Mother Earth,
500
> Thanked God. Too soon. Our prayers all done;
> We were on the ice, crossing the river,
> Racing the rising Sun. We lost.
> Its fire turned ice to water;
> We jostled, choked;
> Those who struggled least died soonest.
> A few survivors. We staggered on,
510
> Dragged ourselves through Thrace, a handful,
> Home at last to Persia: motherland,
> Widowland, stripped of all her sons.
>
> A true tale, told – and a fraction, no more,
> Of all the misery God spat on us.

Exit.

CHORUS LEADER.
   All Persia suffers. Heavy, hard to bear,
   God's hard heel stamps us down.

QUEEN.
   I weep for the army lost.
   O my prophetic dream,
   How clear it was, my lords,
   How false your understanding.   520
   None the less, your advice is good.
   I'll pray to the gods above,
   Make offerings to Mother Earth
   And the dead below:
   Corn, honey, oil from the royal store.
   What's done is done,
   But still we can pray that all may yet be well.
   My lords, it's in your hands.
   Trusted counsellors! If Xerxes comes,
   Speak to him, gentle him, bring him home.   530
   Let no more sorrow tread on sorrow's heels.

   Exit.

CHORUS.
   Zeus, majesty, you took
   Our army, swollen,
   Teeming in its pride,
   And smashed it;
   Took Susa, Agbatana,
   Shadowed them in tears.
   See! Mothers' hands, soft hands,
   Tear clothes for grief,
   Beat breasts, cheeks drenched with tears.
   Grief sisters all.   540
   New widows weep, young brides,
   Drain wells of tears,
   Their husbands lost,
   Soft beds of happiness,
   Sweet youth, all gone.

   With tears we answer,
   Tears for the dear dead, gone.

All Asia weeps, bereft,
Stripped of her men.
550 Xerxes took them, popo-ee,
Xerxes killed them, toto-ee,
Xerxes trusted to barges,
Freighted with doom.
No Darius he:
Prince of all archers,
Blameless, beloved lord.

Soldiers, sailors,
Sailed on wings of death.
560 Ships took them, popo-ee,
Ships killed them, toto-ee,
Ships splintered them.
But his majesty escaped,
We hear, slipped free,
Trod wintry paths,
Ice-plains, came home.

Too late for them,
A-ah!,
Snatched to their deaths,
Ee-yeh!,
570 They tassel the shore,
O-ah!,
Fringe Salamis. Weep for them,
Bite lips, blood flow,
Till heaven hurts to hear.
O-ah!
Howl for them, howl.

Torn by sharp rocks,
A-ah!,
Fingered by waves,
Ee-yeh!,
Nibbled, nibbled,
O-ah!,
By wordless mouths in clean, clean sea.
580 Weep for them, parents,
Children, wives bereft,

O-ah!,
Hear how they died, and howl.

Who in Asia now
Will knuckle to Persian rule,
Pay tribute, crook the knee?
Who'll hug the ground?
Royal power is dead.   590

Keep guarded tongue?
No longer. Freedom's born,
Lifted the yoke of power.
That bloodsoaked soil
Of Salamis, sea-sprayed,
Holds what was Persia once.

Enter QUEEN.[9]

QUEEN.
Friends, seas of misery we sail.
Only one thing's sure. When disaster breaks,
We wallow in terror; when fair winds blow   600
We think our luck will last forever.
Now, for me, all's dark.
The gods have turned away.
Terror, not triumph, roars in my ears.
Fear flutters in my heart.
So I return alone. On foot. No ... majesty.
In my own hands I bring him offerings –
Darius, my son's royal father –
Peace-offerings. The dead need sweetening.
Here's milk, from purest beast expressed;
Honey, flowers distilled;   610
Here's water from sacred spring;
Wine, Mother Earth's most cherished gift;
Olive oil, pungent, pale;
Plaited flowers, Earth's progeny.
Sing, friends. For the dead,
For Darius, his majesty below.
Call his name. Summon him.   620
I'll slake the ground with offerings,
Due honour to the powers who rule below.

CHORUS LEADER.
>Royal lady, Persia's queen,
>Pour offerings to those who sleep below.
>We'll beg the nether powers,
>Despatchers of the dead,
>To smile on us.

CHORUS.
>Great powers, powers of the Underworld –
>Mother Earth; Hermes; Majesty of Death[10] –
630
>Send his soul from dark to light.
>Some remedy he knows, perhaps,
>Knows ruin's cure. Alone of mortals, knows.
>Perhaps, perhaps he'll speak.

>Can he ever – happy that he is,
>Divinity, our lord –
>Hear our wretchedness,
>Pain's litany?
>Must we cry again, again?
640
>Down there, can you hear us, Majesty?

>Mother Earth, lords of all below,
>Free him, all praise, our king:
>Loud-trumpeted,
>Susa's son, divinity.
>Release him to us, whose equal
>Persian soil never yet embraced.

>Dear, dear he was, and dear his tomb,
>Dear the qualities that it enshrines.
>Lord of the Underworld,
>Surging power is yours –
650
>Let him come up, our god, our king.
>Ee-yeh!

>No warriors of ours he killed,
>War-mongering insanity;
>Divinity we called him,
>Wise as god,
>Sure pilot of his men.
>Ee-yeh!

Sire, sire of old,
Come up, be here!
On tomb's high mound
Saffron sandal step,   660
Royal diadem display.
Evil's antidote, Darius, come!
O-ee!

Hear it now, the pain,
Your people's pain.
Lord of our lord, be here.
Hell's dark boils over us.
Our young are gone, are gone.   670
Evil's antidote, Darius, come!
O-ee!

Ai-ee, ai-ee.
We wept, your friends, wept and wept your death.
Why is this happening, dear lord, dear lord?
Whose is the blame?
They're gone,
The galleys, gone,
Unshipped, no ships at all.   680

The GHOST of Darius appears. [11]

GHOST.
   Lords, trusty of the trusty, whose youth was mine,
   Old men of Persia, our state's distracted – why?
   It groans; it's scarred; it's crushed. Our land!
   Her Majesty, here by my tomb:
   I tremble; I accept her offerings.
   You, sirs, crowding, chanting.
   'Rise up, rise up'. I heard; I woke.
   Hard, hard to find the way. The powers below
   Would sooner keep us there than let us go.   690
   Only my majesty unbarred me. I am here.
   But waste no time. My lease is short.
   What evil weighs Persia down?

CHORUS LEADER.
   Majesty. How can I look,

How speak? My lord.
Old fears return.

GHOST.
Up I came, up, drawn by your spells.
Time's short. What would you say to me?
Spare reverence. Speak up.

CHORUS LEADER.
700 Such things. Even to friends,
I'd shrink to speak.
How can I tell my lord?

GHOST.
Since antique fear still strikes them dumb,
You, lady, who shared my bed and now are old,
Stop wailing, dry these tears. Tell me.
What else is human life but pain?
Sea brims with sorrow; it stalks the land,
Haunts mortals, more every day they live.

QUEEN.
You, of all mortals, knew the happiest fate.
710 Each day you lived, you saw the Sun,
Your life was blessed. All Persia called you god.
I envy you in death, who died before the fall.
Hear all of it, Darius, in one brief moment hear.
We're ruined, lord. All Persia's ruined. All.

GHOST.
Some epidemic? Civil war?

QUEEN.
In Greece. Our army perished there.

GHOST.
Which of my sons their general?

QUEEN.
Xerxes, wild Xerxes, who now rules empty sand.

GHOST.
This march, this madness – land, or sea?

QUEEN.
    Two-pronged attack; twin force.   720

GHOST.
    They crossed the sea – such thousands?

QUEEN.
    He yoked the waves, and walked across.

GHOST.
    He tamed the Bosphorus?

QUEEN.
    God helped.

GHOST.
    God stole his mind.

QUEEN.
    Even so. And this is what he did.

GHOST.
    What of his men, who cause these tears?

QUEEN.
    Destroyed at sea; on land destroyed.

GHOST.
    The king's whole army – speared?

QUEEN.
    Why else should Susa weep?   730

GHOST.
    O popo-ee! Our strength, our rock –

QUEEN.
    Our Bactrians, gone. Not a pensioner remains.

GHOST.
    The flower of our allies, scythed!

QUEEN.
    Alone, they say, Xerxes, a handful of men –

GHOST.
    Died? How? Or are they still alive?

QUEEN.

   – by luck reached the bridge that yokes two lands.

GHOST.

   And crossed? Are they safe? Are you sure of that?

QUEEN.

   The report's confirmed.

GHOST.

   O-ee, how soon the oracle comes true:

740   Zeus hurls it on my son.[12] God's purposes!
   I hoped for longer. But when
   We mortals lose control, the gods fall in with it.
   The spring overflows. Death gushes on all I love.
   My son, the brainless boy, crowned folly king,
   Shackled the Hellespont, God's property,
   Changed sea to land – against all nature! –
   Fettered the waves and made men march across.

750   A mortal playing god to gods! My son
   The fool, the fevered mind, possessed.
   Now all the gold, the power I worked to win
   Lies free for all. It's vulture's meat.

QUEEN.

   Bad company he kept, and listened to,
   Wild Xerxes. You won your sons much gold,
   They told him. Your mighty spear. How weak he
      was,
   They said, who puffed himself at home, who spent
   But never earned. So they said, and said again –
   Until he planned this march, this strike, on Greece.

GHOST.

   And so what's done is done, and done to us.

760   The worst. Complete. A mockery forever.
   Our city, derelict! Our land, unmanned!
   Unheard-of, since Zeus decreed this privilege:
   One man to rule all Asia, her fertile flocks,
   His sceptre all-determinant – as Medus proved,
   First warlord. Next, Medus' son
   Capped all his father's work, steered prudent course.

Then third came Cyrus, favourite of the gods,
Blest king of peace for all who loved his rule.
All Lydia, all Phrygia he won,   770
Ionia. God loved him: right ideas made man.
Next, Cyrus' son commanded, fourth in line;
Fifth Mardus, who fouled his fatherland,
Soiled its ancient throne. A palace coup,
Artaphrenes its leader, strong friends,
Loyal hands, did him to death. Lots cast,
Who should be king.[13] The luck was mine:
Campaigns I fought, proud armies led –   780
And brought no blight on this our state.
Now Xerxes rules. My son. He's raw. Raw his ideas,
No mind for all I taught him. My lords,
Who were young with me, be clear on this:
Of all the kings who held this throne,
Not all of us together did such harm.

CHORUS LEADER.
    What now, Darius, lord? It's done, it's done.
    Where steer a reasoned course?
    Your Persians – how can we now survive?

GHOST.
    Don't tangle with Greeks in Greece.   790
    You may outnumber them,
    But the land itself fights for them.

CHORUS LEADER.
    How, fights?

GHOST.
    Starvation sends, to kill huge armies.

CHORUS LEADER.
    A small force then, hand-picked?

GHOST.
    Not even those still left in Greece today,
    Rags of our men, will win safe passage home.

CHORUS LEADER.
    Not cross the straits?
    Not march from Europe, home?

GHOST.

800 A few of many. God's oracle. Trust it,
Exact so far in all that's happened here.
There's more. His hand-picked force,
Left with such swagger, such empty hope,
Is doomed. Where the plain grows lush and green,
Where Asopus' stream plumps rich Boeotia's soil,
The mother of disasters awaits them there,
Reward for insolence, for scorning God.[14]
As they tramped through Greece, shameless,
   shameless,
810 They plundered images, sacked shrines,
Uprooted altars, junked, defiled, debased.
Such sacrilege breeds pain.
They'll pay and pay. Who'll cap
The well of grief? It spouts and spouts.[15]
See! Bloody slaughter scabs Boeotia's soil;
Greek spears pile dead; heaped corpses send
Voiceless messages – to us, our children,
Our children's children.
820 'You're mortal. Don't plume yourselves.
When vanity flowers,
Its fruit is pain, its harvest tears.'
See what they did; their punishment;
Remember Athens, Greece, each time
You think today's good luck not good enough.
Each time you play for more, you'll lose:
Zeus comes down hard on those who grow too
   proud.
830 You're wise, sirs. Use your wisdom.
Teach Xerxes – explain to him –
He must end his pride, his arrogance,
Must not provoke the gods.
As for you, Majesty, mother of my son:
Go in, fetch clothes to welcome him.
Your child. Defeat has tattered him,
Beggared him, ripped finery to rags.
Speak kindly. Gentle him.

Your voice is the only one he'll bear.
Now I return, to the dark below the Earth.
My lords, farewell. In all this grief   840
Enjoy what you have, still have: your life.
Pomp, honour, wealth, are nothing to the dead.

The GHOST *disappears.*

CHORUS.
To hear poor Persia's pain,
Pain now, to come. It hurts!

QUEEN.
God tramples us. Grief swarms.
But worst of all, it stings
To hear how my son, my prince,
Wears tatters, rags.
I'll go, find royal robes.
I'll smile for him.   850
My darling!
I'll not betray him, come what may.

Exit.

CHORUS.
O popo-ee, how great, how good the life
In peaceful times enjoyed!
The days when our old king,
Great governor, who worked no harm,
Allowed no war, our king of kings,
Godlike, Darius ruled this land.

How glittering our armies then!
Our laws high battlements,
Our state steered straight.   860
Home then from foreign wars,
Unscared, unscarred,
Our men marched home to happiness.

Oh the cities he stormed!
He never quit his native land,
Never crossed its boundaries,
Cities on Strymon's banks,

Achelous' mouth, the towns of Thrace,
870 Acknowledged him.

All called him king:
Mainland towns, high-towered,
Far from those lagoons;
Seaside towns, by Hellespont,
By intricate Propontis,
At Pontus' mouth.

880 The islands too, sea-scoured,
Buckled against our shore:
Lesbos, Samos olive-rich,
Paros, Naxos, Mykonos,
Tenos, Andros close to land.

890 Limnos, where Icarus fell,
Rhodes, Cnidos, the cities of Cyprus,
Paphos, Soli, Salamis,
Daughter of that Salamis
Who brings us such tears today.

Ionia, teeming, rich, he ruled,
900 Did as he pleased.
Tireless strength was his –
Elite guards, native regiments,
A wall of warriors.
But now the whole world knows
What God has done to us:
We're crushed, we're smashed, we drown.

Enter XERXES.[16]

XERXES.
Yoh!
Unlucky! I! Spit fate,
910 No hiding, mine!
It bites, it feasts,
Eats Persia,
Pain on pain.
O senators, so old, so wise,
My strength is water.

Zeus! Let me lie with them,
The dead ones.
Death shroud me, close my eyes.

CHORUS.
O-toto-ee, Majesty! Good army,
Proud Persia's high renown,
Squadrons   920
Scythed down, made straw!
Earth cries for her sons,
All dead, for Xerxes dead.
You crammed Hell's jaws with them:
Rank on rank they marched,
Their country's flower,
Master-bowmen, rank on rank,
Ten thousand, a million, gone.
Ai-ee! Who'll guard us now?
Our land, our Asia, Majesty,
Shame! Shame!
Is humbled, on its knees.   930

XERXES.
O-ee. I did it. Our race,
Our land, our fatherland,
I blighted them.

CHORUS.
How can we greet you home?
Our words are bruises,
Our whirling cries.
Take them, all stained with tears.   940

XERXES.
Cry. Shriek. Wail.
Burst ears. Now Fate
Falls full on me.

CHORUS.
We cry, shriek, wail.
Defeat demands. The ships:
Sea drums on them, death drums.
Cry grief, cry pain.

XERXES.

950   Greeks did it, Greeks,
　　Their ships their armour,
　　Ares their armourer,
　　Sculling that midnight sea,
　　That dreadful shore.

CHORUS.
　　O-ee, o-ee, o-ee. Cry out,
　　Ask all the questions.
　　Where are they, where, our sons?
　　Where those who stood by you?
　　Pharandaces,
　　Susas, Pelagon, Agabatas,
960　Dotamas, Psammis, Sousiscanes?

XERXES.
　　I left them. All,
　　Spilled from Tyrian ship,
　　Lurching against the shore,
　　Hard Salamis, pulped
　　On unyielding rock.

CHORUS.
　　O-ee, o-ee, o-ee. Where now
　　Pharnuchus, where
　　Brave Ariomardus, Seualces lord,
970　Lilaeus, Artembares,
　　Memphis,
　　Tharybis, Masistras,
　　Histaechmas? Account for them!

XERXES.
　　Yoh yoh mo-ee,
　　Athens, mouth of hell,
　　They saw, in one last gasp,
　　E-he! E-he!
　　They choked on it.

CHORUS.
　　Was it there, was it there you saw
　　Your eye plucked out,

Alpistus, Eye of Majesty,
Who counted them out, your men,
Your thousands, Batanochus' son?   980
Parthus, son of Sesames,
Great Oebares, Megabates' son –
Did you dump them there,
Oh, oh, oh, da-yohn,
Unmanned great Persia there?

XERXES.
You name my friends,
My dear companions.
Accursed, accursed,   990
Bo-a-ee, bo-a-ee, tear the heart.

CHORUS.
More we need to know. The Mardians,
Their marshal Xanthes,
Anchares Ares' liege,
Diaexis, Arsaces horsetamer,
Lythimnas, Egdadatas,
Tolmus, spearlord who strode in blood –
We name them in tears.
Where are they, where?   1000
Why not here,
Your Majesty's loyal retinue?

XERXES.
They're gone, our warlords, gone.

CHORUS.
Gone, o-ee, no more.

XERXES.
Yay, yay, yoh, yoh.

CHORUS.
Yoh, yoh, great powers,
Fate glared, we fell.
Ruin! How could we know?

XERXES.
Whips bite and bite.

CHORUS.
  It hurts.

XERXES.
1010 New lash. New pain.

CHORUS.
  Greeks of the sea,
  We chanced on Greeks.
  Defeat, disaster, pain.

XERXES.
  Our army, gone.

CHORUS.
  Great Persia, down.

XERXES.
  All's tatters.

CHORUS.
  Rags.

XERXES.
1020 This quiver –

CHORUS.
  You kept it, why?

XERXES.
  My strength, my treasure.

CHORUS.
  So much before, so little now.

XERXES.
  No help. We're naked.

CHORUS.
  Greeks stood their ground.

XERXES.
  I watched. I saw. Disaster.

CHORUS.
  When the warships ran?

XERXES.
I ripped my robes.   1030

CHORUS.
Papa-ee, papa-ee.

XERXES.
Papa-ee, yet more.

CHORUS.
Whips bite and bite.

XERXES.
We mourn. They gloat, our enemies.

CHORUS.
Our strength's sliced off.

XERXES.
I'm naked. Guards, lords, gone.

CHORUS.
Drowned all we love.

XERXES.
Weep, weep, the grief.
Go in and weep.

CHORUS.
Ai-ee, ai-ee, again, again.

XERXES.
Cry out, echo tears with tears.   1040

CHORUS.
A sorry gift for sorrow's sorry sire.

XERXES.
Sing sorrow. Cry my pain.

CHORUS.
Ototo-toto-ee.
It weighs on us;
Your grief, our pain.

XERXES.
Beat, beat your breasts.

Your sobs are my relief.

CHORUS.
All tears are we.

XERXES.
Cry out, echo tears with tears.

CHORUS.
Our voices are yours. We weep.

XERXES.
1050 Lift your voices. Cry.

CHORUS.
Ototo-toto-ee.
Black bruises speak,
Give voice to pain.

XERXES.
Beat breasts. Cry. Howl.

CHORUS.
Pain, pain.

XERXES.
Rip hair from beards. White hair.

CHORUS.
Claw, tear.

XERXES.
Howl.

CHORUS.
We howl.

XERXES.
1060 Tear clothes. Robes. Tear.

CHORUS.
Pain, pain.

XERXES.
Rip hair from head. For them!

CHORUS.
Claw, tear.

XERXES.
Flow tears.

CHORUS.
Tears flow.

XERXES.
Cry out, echo tears with tears.

CHORUS.
O-ee, o-ee.

XERXES.
Home, home in tears.

CHORUS.
Yoh, yoh, each step is pain.   1070

XERXES.
Yoh-ah, down every street.

CHORUS.
Yoh-ah, yoh-ah.

XERXES.
Walk softly. Sob.

CHORUS.
Yoh, yoh, each step is pain.

XERXES.
Ee-ee, ee-ee, the trireme men.
Ee-ee, ee-ee, they drowned, they died.

CHORUS.
Home now. We lead you home in tears.

Exeunt.

SEVEN AGAINST THEBES

Characters

ETEOCLES, KING OF THEBES
SOLDIER
MESSENGER
ANTIGONE
ISMENE
HERALD
CHORUS OF WOMEN OF THEBES
POLYNICES
CITIZENS, SOLDIERS (silent parts)

In front of the palace doors of Thebes. A group of CITIZENS *is waiting for news.*[17] *Enter* ETEOCLES.

ETEOCLES.
    People of Thebes, the hour of fate is now.
    I am your helmsman – this hand to guide
    The state, these eyes that never rest.
    If things go well, thanks be to the gods.
    If they go ill (which heaven forbid),
    One man will be blamed, one name
    Muttered in the city, cursed with groans.
    Eteocles. My name. Zeus Protector,
    Fulfil your name, protect us now.
    I speak to you all:
    Those in the dawn of youth, those whose day is done.   10
    A vital shoot grows in each one of you,
    A sapling of strength. Cherish it!
    Be strong for the city and its gods,
    Respect for them is not to die;
    Be strong for your children;
    For this earth of Thebes,
    The nurse who cradled you,
    Bore all the burdens of your growing-time,
    Reared you to live in her, to fight,
    Be strong for her now. She needs your strength.   20

    So far Zeus has tipped the scales our way.
    A long siege, the enemy always at the walls –
    And the god is with us, so far.
    Now Tiresias, our prophet, speaks:
    Infallible shepherd of the birds,
    Who hears, who tells their omens –
    No need of sacrificial flame.
    Thus, now, he hears, he warns:
    Night-councils in the enemy –
    They plan a huge attack, a final thrust.

    Man the battlements, the entrances. Hurry.   30
    Arm yourselves. Swarm the walkways full,
    The scaffolding towers, the gates. Be brave,
    Stand firm, face all that foreign horde.
    God will give us victory. My spies are out

To track their army – and not in vain:
Their skill my warrant against surprise.

Enter SOLDIER.

SOLDIER.
    Eteocles, captain of Thebes,
40 News of the enemy I bring. Clear news,
    First hand news: I saw it for myself.

    Seven men, warlords, slit a bull's throat,
    Caught its blood in a black-rimmed shield,
    Dabbled common fingers and swore an oath–
    To Ares the wargod, bloodthirsty Fear and Rout –
    Either to smash this city and trample it
    Or paddle our soil with their dying blood.
    Keepsakes they left for their parents at home,
50 Hung on Adrastus' chariot. Tears they wept,
    Yet made no sound of grief. Hearts of iron,
    Courage blazing, war-glow in lion eyes.
    Confirmation treads on the heels of news:
    I left them casting lots how each
    Should lead his men against your gates.

    Our best, our bravest – quickly
    Set them against the gates. Even as I speak
    The Argive army moves nearer, nearer:
60 A dustcloud, flecked foam from horses' lungs.
    Helmsman, use your skill. Reef in your town.
    The storm of Ares blows:
    Waves of soldiers swirl and roar.
    Snatch the moment now.
    For me, count on me:
    Unsleeping eyes, true tongue,
    A fence of news.
    I'll keep true watch.

    Exit.

ETEOCLES.
    Zeus! Mother Earth! Gods of Thebes!

Rabid Fury of Oedipus my father,   70
Spare my city. Never root her up,
Topple, trample her in death.
Our homes, our shrines – we're Greeks,
Free people, Cadmus' children:
Never cast us down in chains.
To arms! To arms! Your cause and ours I plead:
No prosperous state forgets the gods.

Enter CHORUS, *in disorder.*[18]

CHORUS.
Squeal terror, looming fear.
It's loosed, the army. Out of camp.   80
A flood, a dust-swarm,
Marching, galloping. See it! See it!
Tongueless messenger, it tells no lie.
On the plain, our plain, a pulse
A breath of arms.
It's coming, it's coming.
It skims, it flies.
Torrent in mountain gorge.

Yoh! Yoh!
Gods, goddesses, it rears,
Evil, turn it aside.
O-ah!
It hurls on the walls.   90
Surging shields, dazzling,
White shields pound Thebes.
Which god, which goddess?
Who our champion?
Whose altars? Where kneel?
Yoh! Blessed ones, do you hear?

Grab images. Cling.
Cling. Don't wait and howl.
Hear them! Shield-rattle. Hear!   100
Robe the statues,
Crown them now.
I'm afraid. Spear cracks on spear.
Up, Ares! Wargod, Ares, up!

Ancient ally, help us now.
Gold-helmet-god, look down, look down.
You loved us so.

Gods of Thebes come, come gods of this land.
110 We beg you, your faithful ones,
Let us not be slaves.
A wave of men, plumed men,
Breath of the wargod roars on Thebes.
Zeus father, all-powerful,
Snatch vile hands away.

120 The Argives, a ring of men,
War-weapons, terrible.
Bits in horses' teeth
Chink death, chink death.
Seven warlords, captains of men,
With spears and armour stand,
Each gallant at his gate.

Pallas Athene, seed of Zeus,
Whose glory is battle, protect us!
130 Poseidon, sealord, charioteer,
Trident-bearer, snatch our fear.
Ares, show yourself,
Protect us, cherish us:
We're yours, we're yours.

140 Aphrodite, mother of Thebes,
Help us, blood of your blood:
We cling to you,
Our prayers are right, are right.
Wolf-Apollo, be a wolf to them,
Savage them. Artemis,
Daughter of Leto, huntress,
Draw now your bow.

150 E! E! E! E![19]
Squeal of chariots round Thebes I hear.
Hera, queen of heaven.
Tormented axles scream.
Artemis, beloved.
Mad sky, bristling spears.

What will it suffer, our city? What will happen?
What end do the gods demand?

E! E! E! E!
Stones shower on our battlements.
Beloved Apollo,
Bronze shields pound gates.   160
Son of Zeus, send
Consummation, blessed end of war.
Athene, guardian of Thebes, stand close, protect
Your home, the seven gates.

Yoh! Powerful ones,
Gods, goddesses,
On sentry-go for Thebes,
Spear-sick city, betray it not
To a babble of enemies.   170
Hear us, in justice hear us,
Our prayers, our hands outstretched.

Yoh! Powers beloved,
Deliverers, straddle Thebes,
Show your love for Thebes.
Rich rites you had of us,
Feasts of prayer, of sacrifice–
Remember them! Remember
And help us now.   180

ETEOCLES.
Intolerable! Vile creatures!
Is this how you help the city?
Is this the heart you give our men?
Grovelling at images, howling, shrieking,
Outraging decency! Good times or bad,
Who'd live with women?
On top, they're unendurable; done down,
They pull the town around their ears.   190
Our soldiers, look! Scream panic in every street,
You rip the heart from them. Out there
Our enemies laugh; inside we destroy ourselves.
Live with women, that's the price you pay.
Obedience I demand from everyone:

Man, woman, child. Those who disobey
Will be sentenced and stoned.
Death; no reprieve.
200 Affairs of state – men's work! We want
No women here. Go in, do no more harm.
D'you hear me? Go in! Go in!

CHORUS LEADER.
Dear son of Oedipus, we're afraid.
Scrape, squeal of chariots we hear,
Whistle of wheels, twang of bits,
Iron bridles singing in horses' mouths.

ETEOCLES.
Do sailors leave their watch
And huddle in the hold
210 When ships labour in rolling sea?

CHORUS LEADER.
We scrambled to the gods, the old powers,
The images. Hailstorm of rocks
Against the gates. Up, up we ran. Afraid.
To the blessed ones, to beg their help.

ETEOCLES.
Stout walls to blunt Argive spears –
That's the gods' concern. They say:
When a city's captured, its gods abandon it.

CHORUS LEADER.
May I never live to see
220 Our company of gods desert,
The enemy swarm in our streets,
Burning, destroying.

ETEOCLES.
Pray if you will. But remember:
Obedience is mother to Success,
Salvation's consort. People say.

CHORUS LEADER.
People say. But the gods' power
Stands over all. In troubled times,

Hard pain, look up to the gods –
The dark clouds lift.

ETEOCLES.
Men's work to sacrifice, consult   230
The gods, when the enemy's at the gates.
Women, keep quiet and stay inside.

CHORUS LEADER.
Thanks to the gods we live in a city
Unbeaten still. Our walls hold enemies at bay.
Will your anger deny us that?

ETEOCLES.
Honour the gods; that I'll not deny.
But calmly, without panic:
You sow terror in our fighting men.

CHORUS LEADER.
Unheard-of sounds. Discordant prattle.
We fled in fear   240
To the holy place, to pray.

ETEOCLES.
Men will die, be wounded, and you
Will hear of it. But never snatch
At the news with shrieks.
For it is common: Ares the wargod
Feasts on mortals, laps their blood.

CHORUS LEADER.
Horses neighing. I hear them!

ETEOCLES.
Hear quietly, if hear you must.

CHORUS LEADER.
Earth groans, walls groan. They're everywhere!

ETEOCLES.
I'll deal with them.

CHORUS LEADER.
Noise at the gates!

ETEOCLES.

250   Don't blab to all the town.

CHORUS LEADER.
Gods of Thebes, crowd now!

ETEOCLES.
Damn you, be quiet! Have done!

CHORUS LEADER.
Gods of Thebes, don't make us slaves.

ETEOCLES.
You make us slaves: yourselves and all of us.

CHORUS LEADER.
Almighty Zeus, shoot our enemies down.

ETEOCLES.
Zeus: women! What a gift you gave!

CHORUS LEADER.
We suffer like men when the city falls.

ETEOCLES.
Parade gods' images, and speak such words?

CHORUS LEADER.
Fear! Fear! Terror trips my tongue.

ETEOCLES.

260   Do as I say. One favour. Now.

CHORUS LEADER.
What favour?

ETEOCLES.
Have done. Suffer in silence.
Don't panic those you love.

CHORUS LEADER.
No more words.
Like the rest, I'll bow to fate.

ETEOCLES.
That's better. The omen in these words I take.

Now, leave the images. Pray for help,
For the gods to march with us.
Take your words from me. Sing hymns
Of hope, of sacrifice. Greek ritual.
Put heart in those we love; dissolve their fear.   270

Guardians of Thebes,
Gods of farmland and marketplace,
River-spirits of Dirce and Ismenus,
To you these prayers.
When victory is ours, when our city's safe,
Your altars will stream with sacrifice.
Sheep, oxen,
Trophies, spoils of the enemy;
Their tattered armour will scab your shrines.

Make these your prayers. No tears,
No snorts and grunts. Fate is fate: 280
You'll not shriek free of it.

I'll choose six men, myself the seventh,
And station them against the enemy:
Seven champions, each at his gate.
This now. I need no messengers,
No torrent of words to fire my heart.

Exit.

CHORUS.
He speaks; but my mind is on guard for fear.
Dread tenants my soul,
Flickering terror   290
Of the army that rings the town.
So do timid doves
For their nestlings' sake
Tremble at snakes,
Death wreathed in the nest.
They crowd against our walls,
A horde, numberless, a shoal.
What will become of us?
Jagged rocks they hurl,
Hurl on our men.   300

Gods, children of Zeus,
Stretch out,
Save our city, our army,
For Thebes be strong.
What better place on Earth will you make your own
If you surrender to our enemies
The loam of Thebes,
Our river-water,
Purest of all Poseidon,
310   Earth-girdler, pours
For mortals to drink?
Gods of our city, stand firm for Thebes.
On the army outside its walls
Rain havoc,
Mutilation, death,
Let them drop their arms and run.
So honour will be ours –
And you? Warriors,
Deliverers, we'll name you then.
Set firm your thrones,
320   Hear these shrill prayers.

Cause for tears! A city old as time
Packed off to death before it's due.
Spear-spoils, slaves, flakes of ash
Crumbled by fellow-Greeks
While the gods stand by. Unjust!
Its women, its girls, led away,
E! E!, women and girls
Like ponies dragged by the hair,
Clutching their rags.
330   Tears choke in echoing streets,
Empty tears of a people lost.
I shudder at heavy fate.

Cause for grief! Young girls,
Buds of new womanhood unplucked,
Tread paths of bitterness. Slaves!
I say the dead are happier,

Happier far the dead.
For when men break a city,
E! E!, sharp sorrow bites.
Plunder, murder,
Fire-foulness, stench of smoke: 340
Ares the wargod
Pants madness, pants blood,
Smears every shrine with death.

Noise bubbles in the town.
The tower-net tears.
Spears tussle,
Man locks with man.
Babies newborn
Suck blood for milk   350
And wail and wail.
Brothers in plunder
The sackers come:
Full hand calls to full,
Empty to empty hand.
They squabble, they fight;
Each wants more, wants most –
Who can tell the end of it?

Litter of food, stores spilled,
Strewn on the ground:
Wives, weep your tears.   360
Earth's bounty
Trampled, lost.
Slave-girls, new slaves,
New misery, must bed
With new masters now:
The conquerors
Possess their enemies.
Is there hope?
Will the consummation of night
Soothe their sorrow,
Bring comfort in their pain?

CHORUS LEADER.
Look! A soldier. News of the army.

370   He's hurrying, forcing his legs to run.
        Lord Eteocles too, running,
        Running to hear the news.

        Enter ETEOCLES *and* SOLDIER.

SOLDIER.
        I can tell you the exact position of the enemy,
        Which champion has drawn which gate by lot.
        Tydeus at the Proïtis Gate fumes and waits.
        Unfavourable omens –
        The priest forbids him cross the river yet.
380   He's on tiptoe with eagerness, mad to fight,
        Like a sunstruck snake, hissing, spitting insults.
        'So wise,' he snarls at the priest,
        'And gutless! Afraid to fight!'
        So he shouts, and shakes his helmet crests,
        Three crests, a shadow-mane.
        Bronze tassels on his armour rattle terror.
        On his shield-front this arrogant device:
        A sky blazing stars, and on the boss the Moon,
390   Queen of heaven, glittering, eye of night.
        Delirious with arrogance, puffed with arms,
        He roars his battle-hunger on the banks,
        A racehorse at the starting-line, snorting at the bit,
        Rearing at the trumpet call. So Tydeus.
        Who'll face him? When the bolts shoot back
        At the Proïtis Gate, which champion stands for
           Thebes?

ETEOCLES.
        No man's armour frightens me.
        Designs on shields break no man's bones;
        Tassels and helmet-crests don't bite,
400   Don't carry spears. This night-sky you speak of,
        Painted on his shield, a glitter of stars –
        Foolishness, an omen for the man himself.
        His night, his own eyes dark in death –
        A just end to his arrogance,
        Insolent boasting that bites itself.
        Against Tydeus, the champion I choose

Is Melanippus son of Astacus. A noble lord,
Servant of modesty, enemy of arrogance.   410
Shrinks only from evil; brave of the brave.
When Cadmus sowed the dragon-seed in Thebes,[20]
And men grew – he's of that proud stock,
Melanippus of Thebes. The outcome
Is in Ares' hands, a throw of dice:
But Justice, blood of his blood,
Arms Melanippus to fight for his city now.

CHORUS LEADER.
    Gods, give him victory, our champion.
    Justly he fights for Thebes.
    Let us never see their blood,
    Never see them die for those they love.   420

SOLDIER.
    May the gods grant Melanippus victory.
    The second gate, Electra's, was drawn by Capaneus.
    A man-monster, worse than the last.
    Bloated with arrogance, huge threats
    Against the walls – fate cancel them!
    God willing or unwilling he'll topple Thebes,
    He says, fall Zeus's anger where it will.
    Lightning? Thunder? He'll bask in them,   430
    He says, like sunshine after noon.
    His emblem: an unarmed man, fire-bringer,
    A blazing torch held high.
    His motto in gold, 'I'll burn the town'.
    Who'll challenge such a man?
    Who'll hear his threats and never flinch?

ETEOCLES.
    Huffing and puffing: the gain is ours.
    You'll see: balloons of boasts
    The truth soon pricks, the true tongue tells.
    Capaneus threatens deeds, not words alone: 440
    He mocks the gods, sends mortal tongue
    Vaulting to heaven, waves of words
    To spatter on Zeus. Firebringer!
    A thunderbolt will bring him fire,

And nothing like the sun in afternoon.
I set against this blabberer
Lord Polyphontes – a man of fire and strength,
Breastplate of Thebes, champion of Artemis
450   The Protector and other gods.
Name the next gate, and the man they chose for it.

CHORUS LEADER.
Death to the boaster who threatened Thebes!
Send down thunder to stop him dead
Before he breaks in with spear erect
To ravish and pillage my maiden store.[21]

SOLDIER.
Etyoclus was next. From the hammered helmet
The third lot fell to him.
460   He'll hurl his soldiers at the Neïs Gate.
Eager horses, snorting at the bit,
He'll wheel for the attack.
On their cheek-pieces, muzzle-pipes
Play shrill proud music, the breath of war.
On his shield, no mean device he bears:
An armed man on a ladder climbs
The enemy's walls, to tear their town.
His motto, his warcry's written there:
'Not Ares himself can throw me down.'
470   Against him send a champion
Fit to keep slavery's yoke from Thebes.

ETEOCLES.
I'll send Megareus, Creon's son,
Of the dragon-seed. Good luck attend him.
His hands are his boasts: they'll talk for him.
Wild horses! Let them trample the air with neighing,
He'll not flinch from his gate. Either he'll die,
Return to the earth that grew his seed,
Or else he'll take them both, live man
And painted man, with the city on the shield –
A fine trophy to hang in his father's house.
480   Who was next to brag?

CHORUS LEADER.
>Good luck go with him, champion of Thebes,
>Disaster for his enemies. With boasts they come,
>Strutting their craziness against our town.
>See them, Zeus! Judge of all, rage now.

SOLDIER.
>At the fourth gate, close by Athene's temple,
>Hippomedon's vast bulk stands roaring.
>His shield's a sun and moon, a threshing-floor:
>When he whirled it round,
>My hair stood on end for fear.   490
>The device? A giant breathing fire
>And fire's dark brother smoke.
>On the rim, a tangle of snakes
>Twisting, writhing, rivets the framework fast.
>He roars his warcry; he's possessed with war,
>A dervish, drunk for death.
>No easy task, to tackle such a man:
>Terror personified, baying at the gate.   500

ETEOCLES.
>Athene will see to it, who lives beside the gate.
>She'll scorn his boasts; she'll drive him off,
>This snake that threatens chicks and nest.
>And then Hyperbius, Oenops' brave son,
>I'll send against him. Man for man –
>He'll take any risk, put his fate to any test:
>A fine man, his courage and force of arms
>Unquestioned. They're matched, the two of them:
>Personal enemies, and on their shields   510
>Their gods as well are enemies. Firebreathing giant
>Is matched with Zeus enthroned, the Father,
>Thunderbolt flaring in his hand.
>Invincible, Zeus champions our champion.
>So the gods stand on either side. An omen –
>Zeus conquers giant, our man beats theirs.   520

CHORUS LEADER.
>So may it be! On his shield he bears
>Zeus' enemy, Earth-monster,

Bugbear to mortals and gods alike.
Against our gates may he smash his skull!

SOLDIER.

May it be so. Now I tell the fifth, the one
Allotted to the fifth, the Northern Gate,
Hard by Amphion's tomb, the son of Zeus.
He waves a spear and swears by it.
530   Calls it beloved, more precious,
More reliable than God. He waves it and swears
He'll stamp Thebes down in spite of Zeus.
So talks this cub of a mountain mother,
So handsome! Halfway to a man.
Down furs his cheeks: close curls, spring blooms.
Proud heart, man's heart, grim gorgon-eyes.
Parthenopaeus the Arcadian,
Spear-friend of our enemies,
Repays his debt to them with threats on us.
His very shield brags, insults our walls –
540   Full-length, moulded to protect his body,
Its emblem the Sphinx that ate men raw,
Beaten in bronze, riveted in place.
In her claws a Theban, her prey –
An insult that earns him every spear in Thebes.
Wholesaler of death, he'll give no change:
Parthenopaeus the Arcadian,
Stranger reared in Argos,
Who vows to pay the price in Theban blood.
God reject his prayers!

ETEOCLES.

550   God turn their boasts, their insults,
Against themselves.
Deal evil, pain and death.
For this one too, this Arcadian,
We have a man. A quiet man – deeds not words:
Aktor. His actions speak.
Brother of him I mentioned last.
He'll not let such a flow of deedless words
Babble its way inside our gates;
He'll stop that scorpion Sphinx,

Turn it on itself, 560
Stamp it dead outside the walls.
God grant these words, this omen.

CHORUS LEADER.
  Their words stab my heart.
  My hair stands on end.
  They blaspheme, they brag!
  O gods, oh gods,
  Cut them down,
  Kill them for all to see.

SOLDIER.
  Sixth I name an honest man. No braggart:
  A brave man, a priest. Lord Amphiaraus.
  He's stationed at the Homoloian Gate. 570
  Lord Tydeus he accuses,
  Calls him murderer, mischief-maker,
  Evil genius of Argos, mouthpiece of hell,
  Death's minister, who led Adrastus on
  To this madness, this insensate war.
  Another name he tosses in the air: Polynices,
  Lord Polynices, your brother. Again and again
  He names him: portent of death.
  This is what he says: 'A fine thing, dear to the gods, 580
  Glorious forever on mortal tongues:
  Pick up an army, out of town,
  And hurl it at your country, your country's gods!
  Clear water, your motherland – what right have you
  To dam it dry? Your people, put to the sword –
  How do they advance your cause? For my part,
  I mean to enrich this land: my tomb, my oracle
  Will fatten it forever. Come! Fight!
  I'll die with honour, if die I must.'
  So says the priest. His shield held firm. 590
  No emblem he carries: he proclaims
  His honour in what he does.
  His mind is a fertile field,
  Its crop good counsel, common sense.
  Pick well his adversary: a brave man, wise.
  Respect for the gods gives him authority.

ETEOCLES.

A bitter chance it is in human life
That couples honest men with criminals.
Whatever the enterprise, there's nothing worse
600 Than bad companions, dead sea fruit.
The sower folly, the harvest death.
When an honest man
Takes passage with pirates,
God drowns them all, good and bad alike.
Just you may be, but live in a state
That fights its neighbours, forgets the gods –
You're caught in the self-same snare,
The gods scourge all alike.
So this priest now, Amphiaraus –
610 Wise, godfearing, just,
Gifted with prophecy – couples himself
(Commonsense or not) with loudmouthed, godless
    men.
There's no return: he treads a long road down;
He'll fall, be crushed. The will of Zeus.
I think he'll not attack his gate.
Not from cowardice, faintheartedness,
But because he knows his end, his death
In this battle, if Apollo's words bear fruit –
And when Apollo speaks, his words are true.
Nevertheless, against Amphiaraus I send
620 Lord Lasthenes, a surly gatekeeper,
Old in wisdom, in sinew young,
Keeneyed, swift to hurl his spear
In the instant his enemy drops his guard.
For mortals, God alone grants victory.

CHORUS LEADER.

O gods, our prayers are lawful.
Grant them,
Grant victory to Thebes, and turn
On our enemies the scythe of war.
630 Zeus, strike them down outside our walls!

SOLDIER.

Now I'll tell the seventh, at the seventh gate.

Polynices, your own brother.
Curses and death he calls on us.
He swears he'll mount the walls,
Thebes' conqueror proclaimed; he'll chant
His war-whoop, his victory-cry; hand to hand,
Death for death, he'll lock with you –
And if you live, he'll banish you,
Smear you with exile as you dishonoured him.
He calls to witness
Gods of your family, gods of your native land.   640
So the warlord crows.

His shield's brand new – a circle,
Two figures embossed in gold:
A man in armour, a woman leading him
Calmly, modestly. The motto reads, 'Justice I am. I bring
   this exile home
To the city and palace that are his by right.'

Now you know all their purposes.
My report is accurate.
Helmsman, it's for you to choose.   650
What man will you send? You must decide.

Exit.

ETEOCLES.
Cursed house of Oedipus, house of tears,
Possessed, abomination of gods,
My father's curse now blooms in me.
No tears! No tears, for fear
They spawn worse suffering still.
And for Polynices, prince of strife –
Will the motto on his shield speak true?
Will the golden goddess bring him home?   660
He babbles; he's insane. If Justice,
Virgin daughter of Zeus, had ever lain
In his heart or hand, this might have been.
But never once did she smile on what he did:
From the moment he slipped from his mother's dark womb
Through all his childhood, his growing up,
Till the beard of manhood thickened on his chin,

Not once did Justice acknowledge him. And now
He plots rape on Thebes. If Justice stands by,
670   Says yes to this madness, she denies her name.
So I believe.
I'll face the man myself.
Prince against prince, brother against brother,
Enemy against enemy – who has more right than I?
My armour, quickly, to save me from spear and
      stone.

CHORUS LEADER.
No! Dear lord, son of Oedipus,
Don't share his loudness, his craziness.
It's enough that men of Thebes
680   Lock with the enemy: that guilt
Can be washed away. But brother's blood!
Shed that, pollution never fades.

ETEOCLES.
Evil endured without dishonour –
Our only comfort once we're dead.
For who'll praise evil and dishonour mixed?

CHORUS LEADER.
Such haste, my child! Spear-lust,
Whirlwinds of eagerness gorge your mind.
Abort them, end them now.

ETEOCLES.
Whirlwind of the gods, house of Oedipus
690   Full sail on the sea of death,
Apollo's curse. Ride on! Ride on!

CHORUS LEADER.
Sharp hunger bites you:
Bitter banquet, human flesh,
Forbidden blood.

ETEOCLES.
Black curse of Oedipus beloved
Haunts my eyes that will not weep,
Whispers victory and death.

CHORUS LEADER.
    Pay no heed to it! Live as best you can –
    What blame in that? Make sacrifice:
    That black-cloaked Fury will fly away.   700

ETEOCLES.
    The gods have turned from us. One sacrifice,
    One only, will please them now: our death.
    Our future's death – can it be fawned away?

CHORUS LEADER.
    Still there's time. Even now
    The storm of heaven can rage
    More gently. Now it blows full force –

ETEOCLES.
    – stirred up by the curse of Oedipus.
    I dream prophetic dreams: 710
    They parcel and divide my father's state.

CHORUS LEADER.
    This once, accept a woman's words.

ETEOCLES.
    Say what you'd have me do.

CHORUS LEADER.
    Don't go to the gate. Don't walk that road.

ETEOCLES.
    I'm sharp: don't blunt me now.

CHORUS LEADER.
    Give way. The gods approve.

ETEOCLES.
    These are no words for soldier's ears.

CHORUS LEADER.
    You'd harvest your brother's blood?

ETEOCLES.
    God gives us evil: there is no escape.

    Exit.

CHORUS.

720   I tremble for fear. There is
      A Fury, kin to no other power,
      Who feeds on a father's curse.
      A bird of death, brooding,
      Infallible, death to the house.
      Oedipus' raving she'll bring to pass;
      Hatred spur son to murder son.

      A stranger allots them land.
      A harsh judge from the East
      Carves all their goods for them.
730   He's iron, sharp-hearted iron.
      Iron plunders their land,
      Their wide land, and gives to each
      One slice, one narrow grave.

      When they die at each other's hand,
      When dust gulps blood,
      Their black congealing blood,
      Whose then the ritual,
      Whose cleansing hand
      To wash them clean?
740   New evils in the house
      Share tenancy with old.

      Old disobedience I tell,
      Its punishment swift and long –
      Three generations long.
      Apollo spoke, and Laius disobeyed.
      Three warnings Apollo gave,
      Three warnings from the shrine:
      'If you would see Thebes live,
      Then childless must you die.'

750   Unthinking Laius with lust
      Sowed seed of death:
      Oedipus, father-killer,
      Who ploughed the furrow
      Where he himself was sown.
      Harvest of blood he sowed,
      Coupled in madness,
      Bride and groom in rut.

Waves of disaster fall.
They swell, roar, crash
Hard on the city's hull: 760
Thin hull,
Defence no wider than a wall.
I tremble at it.
The kings are foundering –
Must Thebes drown too?

A curse made long ago falls due,
And must be paid. Disaster sees
If people are poor, and passes by.
But the rich, grown sleek and fat,   770
Must empty the warehouse, pay all they have.

What king was ever so admired
By gods, by fellow-citizens,
By the thronging human race,
As Oedipus, that day he killed
The Sphinx who preyed on flesh?

But when he knew at last
His marriage, horror, pain it was.   780
In misery, in craziness,
He did two evils. First
With his own hand, his father-slaying hand,
He took a pin and ripped his eyes,
More to him than his sons.

When his own disowned him then,
He cursed them with savage words:
That one day they would take a sword
And split their inheritance.
Now I tremble. A Fury is upon us,   790
Swift Fury, to see it come to pass.

Enter MESSENGER.[22]

MESSENGER.
    Happiness, daughters of your mothers nursed!
    The threat of slavery is gone; chap-fallen
    The boasts of those mighty men.

We ride at anchor; in all that storm
We let no water in. Thebes' walls,
Its fence of fighting men, stood firm.
At six of the seven gates, all's well.
800   At the seventh, Apollo lord of sevens
Took command; on Oedipus' sons he brought
Full circle Laius' old foolishness.

CHORUS LEADER.
What's happened? More misery for Thebes?

MESSENGER.
Thebes is safe. But the royal brothers –

CHORUS LEADER.
810   Aiee! My prophetic heart!

MESSENGER.
Dead: each at the other's hand,
Squandered by destiny that haunts this house.
My news is happiness and tears:
Happiness for Thebes restored, tears for its princes
Storm-tossed by their father's curse.
They took a sword hammered from Scythian iron
820   And split their inheritance. The land
Is theirs. They lie in it: it sops their blood.

Exit.

CHORUS.
Great Zeus, protecting power
Who stands sentry on the walls of Thebes,
Are we to sing
Songs of thanksgiving, hymns of victory,
Or funeral songs
For our war-commanders dead,
Unhappy princes, last of their line?
True to their names they died –
830   'True glory', 'Much strife' –
Broke heaven's law and died.

Dark destiny, curse fulfilled
For the house of Oedipus.

Ice grips my heart.
I sing them songs of sorrow,
Unhappy brothers,
Bleeding, dying.
A bird of death
Hangs raucous above the spears.

Firm stood the oracle, 840
Unshaken to the end.
Laius defied it, and still it stands.
I am troubled for Thebes:
God's knife is whetted still.
Brothers of sorrow, you did it,
The unheard-of deed you did.
For pity! It's true, no lie.

Soldiers bring in the bodies of ETEOCLES *and*
POLYNICES.

Evidence is here. The messenger spoke truth.
The princes: twinned in anguish, 850
In suffering, in death.
Each killer, each killed.
What words?
Sorrow on sorrow strikes,
Grief tenants the house.

Dear friends, on winds of sighs,
With oarstrokes of hands now send them home,
Black-sailed barge on the river of dark,
To a sunless jetty,
The secret rooms of death. 860

ANTIGONE *and* ISMENE *follow the corpses.*[23]

Look: Antigone, Ismene.
A bitter task is theirs,
Bitter tears for brothers slain.
Soon lovely breasts will swell
With weeping, true tears of grief.
First, we must chant
Threnodies of doom,
Foul triumph-songs of death. 870

Grief-brothered you are,
Most brothered in death of all
Who wear royalty's robes.
I weep: tears unfeigning,
Cries of sorrow that tear the heart.

Stubborn, unyielding,
You pushed to the bitter end,
Sliced with spears your father's house,
A grievous ill.

Grievous men, grievous death,
880   House sheared apart.

Toppled walls,
Thrones of bitterness you saw.
Cold iron your arbiter –
Your quarrel's done.

Your father's curse fulfilled,
The Fury reared and struck.

Pierced to the heart,
890   Brother's heart by brother pierced.
Weep for minds possessed,
Weep for the curse,
Blood matched with blood.

Pierced to the heart,
House and brothers pierced
By rage unspeakable,
Accursed; brothers united
In their father's curse.

900   Tears in the city:
Walls weep, earth weeps
For the men it loved.
For those who come after
Their inheritance waits:
The throne they fought for,
The throne that brought them death.

Their inheritance!
Sharp-hearted in their pride
They divided it,
Iron their arbiter.
'Unjust!' we say
Who loved them once,
Hearts bitter at the god of war.   910

Cut with iron they lie.
Cut with iron
There waits for them – what?
A grave, their father's grave.

Tears weep them home,
Wellsprings of tears
Self-nourishing, unchecked,
That tear the heart.
Weep your tears,
Lay waste your heart in tears   920
For the princes dead.

Speak them this epitaph:
For their citizens,
For rank upon rank of enemies
They played the trick of death.

Ill-starred their mother,
Ill-starred above
All mothers of mortals.
For husband her own son she took;
She bore these sons;
Now they are dead, killed   930
Each by his own brother's hand.

Brothers sown of one seed,
Dead of one death;
Sharp-edged they lived,
Mad for jealousy they died.

Their quarrel's done;
Their blood runs common in the dust;

940 True brothers now they are.
 A judge came from the East,
 Sharp-glittering, born of fire:
 Iron, their arbiter. And Ares came
 To divide their spoils, their inheritance,
 Impartial Ares, hard in his hand
 Their father's curse.

 Fate's dice are thrown;
 Grievous their luck from God.
 Rich earth is theirs,
950 Unfathomed riches of the grave.

 See! Gardens of grief you sowed,
 Flowers of misery for all your race.
 Final victory, shrieks of joy, belong
 To the Curses who won the day.
 Scattered, scattered your race;
 Over that gate, your battleground,
 Flutter flags of doom;
 Your demon struck you down,
960 Both down – and now he rests.

ANTIGONE.[24]
 You were struck; you struck.

ISMENE.
 You killed; you were killed.

ANTIGONE.
 With spear you killed.

ISMENE.
 With spear you died.

ANTIGONE.
 Grief you gave.

ISMENE.
 You were given grief.

ANTIGONE.
 Fall sigh.

ISMENE.
 Fall tear.

ANTIGONE.
Slayer.

ISMENE.
Slain.

ANTIGONE *and* ISMENE.
Ee-ay, ee-ay.

ANTIGONE.
Mind reels with grief.

ISMENE.
Tears tear the heart.

ANTIGONE.
Brother of sorrow.

ISMENE.
Brother of grief.

ANTIGONE.
Your loved one you killed.

ISMENE.
By your loved one killed. 970

ANTIGONE.
Two to tell.

ISMENE.
Two to see.

ANTIGONE.
Sorrow on sorrow laid.

ISMENE.
Brother with brother dead.

CHORUS LEADER.
Destiny, grief-giver,
Shadow of Oedipus,
Black Fury,
Great is your power.

ANTIGONE *and* ISMENE.
Ee-ay, ee-ay.

ANTIGONE.
Bitter pain; eyes flinch.

ISMENE.
The exile home.

ANTIGONE.
980   He killed; he came not home.

ISMENE.
Home he came, and panted death.

ANTIGONE.
He died.

ISMENE.
He killed.

ANTIGONE.
Death to see.

ISMENE.
Death to tell.

ANTIGONE.
Death brothered in death.

ISMENE.
Brimming, fluttering pain.

CHORUS-LEADER.
Destiny, grief-giver,
Shadow of Oedipus,
Black Fury,
Great is your power.

ANTIGONE.
In suffering you learned.

ISMENE.
990   You learned, you suffered too.

ANTIGONE.
When you came home to Thebes.

ISMENE.
To challenge him with the spear.

ANTIGONE.
House of grief.

ISMENE.
Unhoused in grief.

ANTIGONE.
Yoh misery.

ISMENE.
Yoh suffering.

ANTIGONE.
For the house.

ISMENE.
For Thebes.

ANTIGONE.
For me.

ISMENE.
For me.

ANTIGONE.
Eteocles, prince of grief.

ISMENE.
Polynices, most racked of men.   1000

ANTIGONE.
God-haunted, blind you were.

ISMENE.
Where shall we bury them?

ANTIGONE.
Where honour lies.

ISMENE.
Bedfellows of their father's pain.

Enter HERALD.[25]

HERALD.
I am to announce the decision and decree
Of the counsellors of Thebes. In recognition

Of his loyalty, his patriotism,
Eteocles is granted burial here
In the earth he loved. For Thebes he died,
Fighting Thebes' enemies. To our ancestral gods
1010 He is without sin or guilt. He died
As young men ought, where honour is.
So stands the decision concerning him.
As for his brother Polynices, his corpse
Is to lie unburied, for dogs to tear.
A fitting end. He'd have toppled Thebes,
But the gods stopped him in his brother's spear.
He's dead; his guilt lives on,
His scorn for our gods.
Foreigners he led against his town.
1020 Scorn and shame are his, well earned;
His grave a vulture's craw. For him
No high-heaped tomb, no funeral dirge,
No ritual of death from next of kin.
So decree the counsellors of Thebes.

ANTIGONE.
Take them this answer, the counsellors.
If no one else will help,
I'll bury him alone, take the risk alone.
My brother! Should I blush
1030 At this rebellion, this disobedience?
Fearful bonds we have:
Our mother's misery, our father's guilt.
His choices are over; now I make my choice –
I stand by him now, living with dead.
No hollow-bellied wolf will tear his flesh,
Decree or no decree. Woman I am,
And woman I'll contrive his grave.
In my rich gown I'll carry earth for him;
1040 I'll cover him; no decree shall turn me back.
I'll do it, never fear. I'll find a way.

HERALD.
I warn you, don't disobey the state.

ANTIGONE.
Don't waste your words.

HERALD.
The people's mood is harsh now danger's past.

ANTIGONE.
Harsh let them be: I mean to bury him.

HERALD.
An outcast! You'll show him such respect?

ANTIGONE.
Did not the gods respect him once?

HERALD.
Before he threatened Thebes.

ANTIGONE.
Ill-treated, he paid ill-treatment back.

HERALD.
No private quarrel! He threatened us all.   1050

ANTIGONE.
Ruin, last of gods, now ends the tale.
I'll bury my brother. Have done with words.

HERALD.
Do as you will. But stand warned by me.

Exit.

CHORUS.
High-necked Furies, demons of death
That haunt this house,
Root out the house of Oedipus,
What can we do?
What act? What punishment?
How can we bear it?
How not weep for you,
Not lay you in the grave?
I'm afraid, I shrink   1060
From the people's rage.
Many you'll find to mourn,
Eteocles; but he must go alone,
Unmourned, save by his sister's tears.

Who could consent to that?

In two separate groups.

Let the state do what it will
To those who mourn for him.
We'll go in procession now
And bury him. This sorrow strikes
1070   All Thebes – and what the state calls just
Shifts, changes from day to day.

With Eteocles now we go,
By justice and state approved.
With the blessed gods, with Zeus
He took the helm, saved us
From drowning in that foreign flood,
Steered us clear of death.

Exeunt.

SUPPLIANTS

Characters

DANAUS
KING OF ARGOS
EGYPTIAN CAPTAIN
SOLDIERS (silent parts)
CHORUS OF DANAUS' DAUGHTERS
CHORUS OF ARGIVE WOMEN

A grove of trees and a meadow, outside the walls of Argos.
Standing stones; images of gods. Enter DANAUS *and the*
CHORUS.[26]

CHORUS.

    Zeus protector, hear us, smile on us.
    From dusty dunes we sailed,
    Nile's jaws; we left your land,
    Green meadows at desert's edge,
    Exiles. No blood-guilt,
    No sentence of banishment,
    No city's will – we chose it,
    Ourselves we chose it,
    Ran from incest,
    Rape-marriage with Aegyptus' sons.   10

    For Danaus, our father, counsellor,
    Leader, on the chessboard of grief
    One gambit remained:
    Keen flight across the sea,
    Landfall in Argos
    Where our race began (they say)
    From distracted Io, quickened
    By the breath and touch of Zeus.
    What other land in all the world
    Should welcome us,
    Suppliants, olive twigs in hand?   20

    O city, earth of Argos, white water,
    Sky gods, gods of Earth beneath –
    And saviour Zeus above all,
    Watchdog of the faithful –
    We beg you: help us,
    Breathe pity on us,
    A summer breeze. But on them,
    Aegyptus' sons, that swarm of men
    Hard-arrogant, send death.   30
    No toehold on these marches:
    Let them gallop the wild sea,
    Thunder, lightning, anvils of wind –
    Let them gulp the storm, and die.
    Hot for our beds,
    They want it! They want it!

Cousin-rape – prevent them now.

40 Now I name
Zeus's calf:
Sea-stranger, browser,
Avenger, child
Of Io, mother of our race
In the breath of Zeus:
Foretold by fate
His name Epaphus, Caress.

Him I name,
50 Recalling Io's suffering,
Race mother, here
In these fields. Clear proof
I'll offer the people,
Unlooked-for truth,
A long tale told at last.

If there are countryfolk,
Bird-watchers who hear these tears,
These sharp tears, they'll think it
60 The nightingale's voice, Tereus' queen,
Hawk-hunted, full of tears.

Here in green countryside
She sobs, full-hearted grief,
Sets out the manner of his death,
Her son: rage pulsed in her heart
And she killed her son.[27]

Like the nightingale, all tears,
With Eastern shrieks
70 We ravage our soft cheeks,
Our hearts unused to grief.
Flowers of tears we pluck;
Terror blooms in us.
Who will help us, cherish us,
Exiles from a misty land?

Marriage-gods, hear! Smile on justice.
80 Their hard young lust,
Break it! Hate their pride!

Marriage with honour grant us now.
From the talons of war
There is refuge, an altar,
A safe rock, a citadel:
Honour the gods, and all is well.

Who knows the will of Zeus?
May it be seen, may it be done.
It blazes, in the black dark
It blazes; mortal fate is there.   90

Zeus nods, and it is done,
Sure-footed, safe.
Dark thickets of thought
Beyond our vision, secret ways.

From their towers of hope
He hurls proud mortals down
Without effort, without arms –
All's easy for the gods.   100
His will, enthroned, is done.

Let him see their arrogance,
Green twig on ancient stem,
Throbbing, thrusting, the pulse of lust:
Delirium goads them, frenzy,
Delusion, charioteer of pain.   110

Pain, tears; tears and pain;
Shrill voices break for grief;
Ee-ay, ee-ay,
Flowers of sorrow,
My living tears my honouring.

Argos, hills of Argos, hear
Shrill, foreign cries.
Ee-ay, ee-ay,
Again and again,   120
Veils rent to rags.

Death's at bay? All's well?
Then pay the gods their due.
Yoh, yoh,

Uncharted seas,
Stormwinds of misery.

Argos, hills of Argos, hear
Shrill, foreign cries.
130 Ee-ay, ee-ay,
Again and again,
Veils rent to rags.

So far oars
And ship's womb,
Linen-wrapped against the waves,
Have brought us.
Fair winds. So far.
Zeus, who sees, who knows
In the crevices of time,
140 Grant us safe harbour now.

Seed of Zeus, holy Io's seed,
Safe harbour we seek,
Free from men's lust,
Unraped virginity.

Artemis,
Virgin daughter of Zeus,
Smile on our smiles,
Virgin Artemis, who keeps the gate,
Unconquered, all-conquering,
150 Huntress, keep us safe,
Snatch us safe from the chase.

Seed of Zeus, holy Io's seed,
Safe harbour we seek,
Free from men's lust,
Unraped virginity.

If not, then down
To the dark landlord below
Of the teeming dead
We'll pray these prayers:
160 Dead in a woven noose,
By gods above betrayed.

Zeus, hear! For Io, for Io,
Still it stirs, it hunts,
Hera's jealous anger:
Stormwinds blow, and bite.

Can Zeus hate him?
Unjust! Unjust! Hate Io's son,
His own loins' son?[28]   170
Can he turn away,
Not heed our prayers? No! No!
He must hear us, hear us on high.

Zeus hear! For Io, for Io,
Still it stirs, it hunts,
Hera's jealous anger:
Stormwinds blow, and bite.

DANAUS.
Children, be cunning. You sailed here
With an old fox for captain. Your father. Me.
Now, on dry land, I'll keep a father's care,
Give you good guidance. Write it in your hearts.
Look – dust. Without words, it says   180
An army's coming. Soon we'll hear axles hiss.
I see a swarm of men: shields, spears,
Horses, chariots. The princes of Argos –
They've heard we've landed, they've come to see.
Is it friendly, this army, or sharp for war?
No matter.
Stay here, girls, here by the stones.
Let gods be our champions, let them decide:
An altar's better than battlements, a solid shield.   190
Come here, quickly. Arrange yourselves.
Twigs in your left hands, as custom is,
Wound with white wool, to show that Zeus
Protects you. Speak when you're spoken to:
Respectful, tearful, as strangers should be –
These people must understand:
You're exiles, yet guilty of no crime.
Quiet voices, downcast looks,

200   No flirting – the people of Argos
      Are easy to offend. Be submissive.
      You're strangers, exiles, in need;
      Royal arrogance sits ill on beggars' lips.

CHORUS LEADER.
      Wise words, father, spoken to the wise.
      We'll store your advice, remember it.
      May Zeus our ancestor look down on us.

DANAUS.
      May he so indeed, with kindly eye.

CHORUS LEADER.
      If he so wills, all may yet be well.

DANAUS.
      Hurry, then. You know what's best to do.

CHORUS LEADER.
210   We'll gather round you, sit at your side.
      Zeus, pity our suffering: save us from death.

DANAUS.
      Zeus' eagle. Pray to him.

CHORUS LEADER.
      On the Sun's life-giving rays we call.

DANAUS.
      Lord Apollo too, once exiled by the gods.

CHORUS LEADER.
      He shared this misery; he'll understand.

DANAUS.
      He'll answer your need, and stand by you.

CHORUS LEADER.
      Should we pray to other gods?

DANAUS.
      This trident, look: a symbol.

CHORUS LEADER.
      Poseidon helped us here: may he help us still.

DANAUS.

    And Hermes too, here in Greek form.   220

CHORUS LEADER.

    Hermes, messenger, bring news of hope.

DANAUS.

    To all the gods at this one altar pray.
    Settle here, in sanctuary: doves
    Huddling from hawks.
    Blood-cousins, polluting kin –
    If bird eats bird, how can it be pure?
    And marriage-rape, against my will and yours –
    How can that be pure? Let them hide
    In the Underworld, they'll hide in vain
    From the guilt of this, if this they do.
    For even in the Underworld, they say,   230
    A second Zeus is there,
    To punish guilt and judge the dead.
    Now remember, answer as I advised
    And all will yet be well.

    Enter KING *with* SOLDIERS.

KING.

    Where are you from?
    A murmur, a ripple of silk, veils ...
    Greeks you are not: what woman of Argos,
    What Greek, wears clothes like these?
    How did you come? How did you dare,
    Unheralded, without guides or friends,
    Without fear? I'm amazed.   240
    Suppliant branches, here at the gods' feet
    As custom demands: that much is clear, and Greek.
    But I'll not guess the rest:
    You must speak, and answer me.

CHORUS LEADER.

    Our clothes, these branches: you're right.
    And you – how shall I address you?
    Private citizen, spokesman, head of state?

KING.

    Answer me with confidence.

250   I am Earth-seed,[29] Ancient, king.
        My people's name:
        Pelasgians, who reap this land.
        Over all the rich plain
        Where the River Strymon flows red in the setting
            sun,
        I am king; over all the land
        From barbarian mountain-lairs
        On Pindus and Dodona, clear down to the sea,
        I am king. And this land here,
260   This ground, is Apia:
        Named after Apis the bull-king,
        Prophet, healer, Apollo's child.
        From Naupactus he sailed,
        And from dragon-plague,
        Foul serpents swarming
        In angry blood of Mother Earth polluted,
        He saved our land. With a surgeon's skill
        He cut, he cauterised – and now
270   He's honoured forever, forever in our prayers.

        So much, and I have done. Now you
        Must tell your lineage. And briefly –
        In Argos we like our speeches short.

CHORUS LEADER.
        Short, then, and clear. Argive birth
        We claim, calves of fertile cow.
        There's proof; I'll tell it plain.

KING.
        Argives? You claim Argive blood?
        How can I believe it?
280   You look like Libyans, not Greeks:
        Children of the Nile, perhaps,
        Or from Cyprus, where craftsmen
        Stamp images like yours on coins;
        Or nomad-women I've read about,
        Camel-riders, neighbours of Africa.
        With bows and arrows
        I'd think you Amazons,

Manless women, who gorge on flesh.
But – Argives? How? Explain.   290

CHORUS LEADER.
There was a priestess in Argos once:
Io, Hera's servant, keeper of keys –

KING.
It's a well-known tale.

CHORUS LEADER.
Zeus slept with her – mortal with god.

KING.
They tangled, yes. And Hera knew.

CHORUS LEADER.
Royal jealousy! What came of it?

KING.
Queen Hera changed Io into a cow.

CHORUS LEADER.
So Zeus – Zeus and the horned cow –   300

KING.
Coupled. He made himself a bull.

CHORUS LEADER.
How did hard Hera answer?

KING.
She set a watchman with a thousand eyes.

CHORUS LEADER.
Which cowherd has a thousand eyes?

KING.
Argus; earth-child. And Hermes cut him down.

CHORUS LEADER.
Did Hera still torment the unhappy cow?

KING.
She sent a fly, a living goad –

CHORUS LEADER.
Gadfly, its Egyptian name.

KING.
    It drove her, in exile, a long wandering.

CHORUS LEADER.
310   Your story fits mine exactly.

KING.
    She came to Canopus, and Memphis too.

CHORUS LEADER.
    Zeus caressed her there, and begot his son.

KING.
    Who claims to be this ... calf of Zeus?

CHORUS LEADER.
    Epaphus – named for the touch of Zeus.

KING.
    And he begat – ?

CHORUS LEADER.
    Libya, who harvests half the world.

KING.
    And her son – ?

CHORUS LEADER.
    Baal Two-sons, our grandfather.

KING.
320   And your father's distinguished name?

CHORUS LEADER.
    Danaus. His brother had fifty sons.

KING.
    And *his* name? Don't hesitate.

CHORUS LEADER.
    Aegyptus. Now you know all our lineage.
    We're Argives. Acknowledge it, help us now!

KING.
    Indeed, you seem to have an ancient right
    To citizenship. But why did you leave
    Egypt, your father's home? What drove you here?

CHORUS LEADER.

    Lord,
    Human suffering flies on iridescent wings:
    No two feathers show alike. Who could guess   330
    This sudden flight from hideous rape
    Would bring landfall in Argos, with our own kith and kin?

KING.

    You're suppliants at the gods' altars;
    You hold raw branches white with wool.
    What is it you ask?

CHORUS LEADER.

    Not to be slaves to Aegyptus' sons.

KING.

    Because you hate them, or because it's wrong?

CHORUS LEADER.

    Of course it's wrong! To be your own kinsman's slave!

KING.

    Intermarriage breeds wealth –

CHORUS LEADER.

    It breeds suffering, and slick divorce.

KING.

    As I honour the gods, how must I help?   340

CHORUS LEADER.

    Never give us up to Aegyptus' sons.

KING.

    And shoulder war? A heavy load.

CHORUS LEADER.

    With Justice your champion –

KING.

    If she was present from the start.

CHORUS LEADER.

    Respect the gods who steer your state.

KING.

    Your branches shadow them; I'm afraid.

CHORUS LEADER.

>Zeus, god of suppliants, is hard if you refuse.
>Earth-child,
>In kindness, in friendship, hear.

350

>We're exiles, on the run:
>Calves, wolf-hunted,
>Quarried on jagged rocks.
>Be our brave herdsman. Hear!

KING.

>In branch-shadow
>The gods beckon.
>I see them. God grant
>No strife from this alliance,
>No war. Unasked! Unasked!
>What city thanks god for that?

CHORUS LEADER.

>Zeus casts his lots upon the world.

360

>May Justice, his daughter,
>Who protects suppliants, send no war.
>Majesty, wise in your years,
>Learn from us, the later-born.
>Respect for suppliants! What greater gift
>Can good people give their gods?

KING.

>If you'd come to me,
>To my private house,
>For sanctuary ... Now the risk
>Is for all the people:
>Theirs the danger, theirs the cure.
>I must consult before I act.

CHORUS LEADER.

370

>*You* are the people! *You* are the state!
>Who dares judge the king?
>You hold the hearth; you tend the fire;
>Your nod, your vote,
>Your sovereignty enthroned
>Guides, guards. Guard now!
>God's anger –

KING.
  – turn on my enemies!
  If I help you, I pay the price;
  If I refuse, I pay the price.
  What should I do? Intervene?
  Leave it to fate? Either way, I fear.   380

CHORUS LEADER.
  Be careful! Look up!
  He's there: watchdog, guardian
  Of those who ask help from kin
  And get it not. The anger of Zeus,
  Protector of suppliants, is on watch
  For those who hear cries for help
  And turn away.

KING.
  What if Aegyptus' sons are right?
  Close kinsmen! If law gives them the right
  To master you, who can deny their claim?
  You must stand trial, and win,   390
  By the laws of the land you left.

CHORUS LEADER.
  No *man* our master! God grant it,
  Law or no law. From frowning rape
  We run, we quarter the Earth,
  We course the stars. Choose justice!
  Approve what the gods approve!

KING.
  Choose me no choices; judge me no judge.
  I said before: I'll not act in this,
  King or no, without the people's voice.
  Suppose fate turned sour?
  'You helped strangers,' they'd say,   400
  'Helped strangers and smashed the state.'

CHORUS LEADER.
  Zeus holds the balance:
  Our ancestor, ours and theirs.
  An impartial judge. For wickedness

The reward is suffering, for goodness, joy.
The scales are poised. Choose justice –
Why do you hesitate?

KING.
What way is best? We need counsel,
Fathoms deep, a clear-eyed diver
Plunging the depths. A straight road
410   For the city, for me. We want no war,
No reprisals from Aegyptus' sons;
But you are suppliants, too –
We can't surrender you
And risk Zeus the Avenger,
Whose hard hand not even Death shakes free.
We need good counsel. Say you not so?

CHORUS (*separate voices*).
Take counsel – and protect us
420   As justice demands. Do not betray us,
Exiles, fugitives,
Prey of godless men.

Let them not spoil us,
Rape us from sanctuary;
Look on those lustful men
And remember god.

Suppliants we are. Let them
430   Not tear us from the gods' embrace,
Lead us like colts to the breaking,
Haltered in silk.

Know this: for whatever you do
Justice will bring recompense
On your children and all your house.
The justice of Zeus: take heed.

KING.
I heed it. My thought is gravelled fast
In war: huge war, necessary war
On one side or the other. It must be so:
440   The hull is pegged, lashed tight;

No landfall now, exempt from pain.
When wealth is plundered from a house
Zeus, if he will, can set things right again.
When the tongue shoots hurtful arrows
Another speech can soften pain:
But to kill one's kin! Blood-guilt!
Avoid it with all sacrifice,   450
Myriad offerings to myriad gods.
This dispute withers me:
I'd rather know nothing
Than know the pain to come.
It must be so; let it not be so.

CHORUS LEADER.
One argument more: the last.

KING.
What is it?

CHORUS LEADER.
Breast-bands and cords we have –

KING.
Women's stuff. No surprise in that.

CHORUS LEADER.
And from them, look! a fine device –

KING.
What d'you mean?   460

CHORUS LEADER.
Unless you promise –

KING.
What will your cords devise?

CHORUS LEADER.
New offerings to deck these gods.

KING.
A riddle: untangle it.

CHORUS LEADER.
From the gods' statues we'll hang ourselves.

KING.
Word-whips: they sting the mind.

CHORUS LEADER.
Your eyes are open. Now you see.

KING.
I'm wrestled to the ground,
Choking in a flood,

470   A fathomless, chartless sea.
No anchorage. I must help you
Or risk pollution beyond all speech.
I must stand against Aegyptus' sons,
My own kinsmen. Foul battle with fouler price:
Men's blood, puddles of blood, for women spilled.

And Zeus' hand is here,
Protector of suppliants.
His shadow is our fear. We bow.

480   Old man, Danaus, gather up
Your daughters' branches in your arms,
And place them in Argos' shrines:
Clear proof to the citizens
That you come as suppliants. Otherwise
There will be arguments –
These people are sharp against authority.
They may even be moved to pity you,
Seeing these branches, to hate
The arrogance of that armada of men.
They may be moved to help –
Such helplessness makes every mortal kind.

DANAUS.
490   We've found a glittering prize:
A champion who fears the gods.
Give me an escort, guides
To show me the temples of the city gods,
To guarantee safe passage.
Look we not like the foreigners we are?
Egypt and Argos breed different stock.
Caution is best: over-confidence

Gives birth to fear; we kill
The friend we fail to recognise.

KING (*to* SOLDIERS).
Go with him; this is good advice.   500
Take him to the city shrines –
And no gossip. He's a sailor;
Take him to the gods' hearth; no more.

Exeunt DANAUS *and* SOLDIERS.

CHORUS LEADER.
He's gone, with your instructions.
What of us? What have we to do?

KING.
Leave your branches here, tokens of need.

CHORUS LEADER.
It's done.

KING.
Move down to level ground.

CHORUS LEADER.
Away from the altars? How is that safe?

KING.
No birds' beaks will tear your flesh.   510

CHORUS LEADER.
Snakes! They're worse than snakes.

KING.
Speak calmly; my words are calm.

CHORUS LEADER.
When terror flutters in our hearts –

KING.
There's nothing to fear.

CHORUS LEADER.
Your words, your deeds, must make it so.

KING.
You'll not long be fatherless.

I'll call the people together,
Persuade them to kindness,
And tell your father what words to use.
520   Wait here, and pray to these gods
To bring you your hearts' desire.
I'll do all I can;
Now may Persuasion guide my tongue,
Good fortune bring all to pass.

Exit.[30]

CHORUS.
Lord of lords, blest of the blest,
Power of all powers, Zeus, richness,
Hear us. Kinsman, hear!
Banish their lust – hated! hated! –
Drown them in purple sea,
530   The pursuers, the swarthy ones.

Look on us, smile down on us,
Women. A long line, an ancient tale:
Remember it! Remember her,
Io, race-mother: you caressed her once.
Proud descent we claim
From Zeus, and this our motherland.

Old tracks, old footprints:
We come from exile home.
540   Here in these meadows
She browsed, she was watched,
The gadfly stung and stung.
Headlong then, mind awry, she ran,
Stampeded, fate's furrow sliced
Across continents,
Headlong, across the sea.

Headlong, headlong,
Arrow in wilderness,
Scatter of sheep,

Trample towns, markets,   550
Headlong, peaks, folds of hills,
River valleys, clear water,
On, on, brown fields, wheat,
The earth, the rich earth,
Headlong, on,

Stampede, stampede, the gadfly goad,
To Egypt, oasis of Zeus,
Fertile land that quaffs the snow,
That flinches in the storm,   560
And the Nile, the pure Nile.
So she ran, the crazy one,
Hera's bacchant, panting pain.

They watched her, the people, the Egyptians,
White-eyed, they watched.
Apparition! Monster! Crazy thing!
Cow? Woman? They watched and watched.   570
Who soothed her then? Who rested her,
Far-ranging, fly-blown,
Ragged Io, the crazy one?

All-powerful, eternal Zeus.
Gentle in strength, with god's breath
He rested her, washed clean
Her shame, her suffering.
He thrust – no lie! – and soon   580
A sinless son she bore

Eternal, ever blest. The earth
Cries aloud with a single voice,
'No lie! No lie! This race
Is Zeus' race, who sows all life,
Who cured the sly witchcraft Hera sent.'
No lie! Zeus' race are we.

On which of the gods   590
More justly should we call?
Zeus gardener, Zeus architect,
Who sowed, who fashioned us,
Who breathes his life in us.

No puppet king,
No shadow-prince
Throned in another's fee.
He is thought made deed:
He speaks, it's done.

Enter DANAUS.

DANAUS.
600   Children, good news. The people ...
In full assembly ... the vote is ours.

CHORUS LEADER.
Father! Your message beggars hope.
The exact words, tell us their words.
Acclamation, yes – but what decree?

DANAUS.
In all Argos, not one dissenting voice.
My heart leapt like a child's.
Thicket of hands, unanimous for us!
What words? These. We can settle here
610   Free of reprisals, free of all pursuit;
No citizen or foreigner has claims on us.
If they try force, our enemies,
Protection's guaranteed:
Any citizen of Argos who fails us
Will pay with banishment. Those are the words.
And his Majesty? With eloquence
He spoke of Zeus, lord of suppliants,
His hungry rage if they should disobey:
Sickness in the city, pollution beyond all cure,
620   A cancer, a feast of pain.
No more call for oratory:
They lifted their arms and voted yes.
Supple words persuaded them –
And Zeus, who brought these things to pass.

CHORUS LEADER.
Sisters, sing blessings for Argos:
Good prayers for good gifts received.
Zeus, lord of host and guest,

Fulfil our words, guest-words,
Blameless and true.

CHORUS.
Gods, hear us, children of Zeus: 630
Full-hearted offerings we pour.
May fear never snatch this land,
Raucous Ares, flesh-harvester,
Never reap this people,
Never dance his dance.

For they pitied us –
Their votes, their voices –
Pitied the suppliants of Zeus,   640
His huddled flock.
Not for men their votes,
Disdaining women's spite.
Zeus' hand in this they saw:
Watchdog, avenger,
Shadow haunting the house –
Who, willingly, calls him down?   650
They pitied us,
Kinswomen, suppliants of Zeus;
Untainted offerings now
They'll give the gods.

From mouth's dark shadow-cave
Bright prayers fly forth.
Gods, send no plague
To gut this land,   660
No civil war
To crimson fields with death.
Let its youth flower free,
Its blooms unharvested
By Ares, reaper of flesh,
Who shares Aphrodite's bed.

Let its altars blaze
With the wisdom of the wise,
God-fearing citizens   670
Who honour Zeus, Zeus above all,
Protector of strangers

Who keeps the old, wise law.
For the land we pray
New guardians; for mothers
In labour, kind Artemis
Who keeps the gate.

680
May never civil war
Rip this land apart;
Let hoarse Ares, unsinger,
Tear-breeder,
Never croak in bronze,
Never dance his dance.
May never sour disease
Swarm on these children,
The people's cubs –
Wolf-Apollo, smile on them!

690
Grant fertile fields,
Lord Zeus; grant fruits
In their season, calves
To each grazing cow;
Protecting powers
Grant every prayer.
Songs of praise and joy
From every altar rise,
God-fearing throats send forth
The voice that loves the lyre.

700
Keep safe the great prerogative,
Wise counsels, the people's rights
That rule the state; to strangers
Grant justice, fair hearing,
No swords unsheathed.

Honour the gods who keep the land;
Bring laurel, make sacrifice,
Hecatombs of praise, as your fathers did.
Honour your parents: in Justice's book
The third great law.

DANAUS.
Good prayers, children. I second them.   710
Summon now your courage: I have news,
Unlooked-for news. Here from sanctuary,
From this high rock, I can see their ship.
No doubt of it. Every detail's plain:
Side-screens, Egyptian sails, a quick eye
Painted on the prow, a steering-oar astern.
They mean no love to us. I can see men:
White clothes, dark limbs. Behind them   720
A whole armada comes. The leaders are close inshore:
Sails furled; a rattle of oars; they land.

Face them calmly; remember the gods.
For my part, I'll go for help,
For advocates to plead our case with steel.
Whoever comes from *them*,
One herald with arguments or soldiers
To snatch, to grab, fear nothing:
They'll not lay hands on you.
If we are slow, if human help is slow,   730
Remember the gods: their power is here.
No human agency sets time aside:
When mortals defy the gods, they're marked to die.

CHORUS LEADER.
Father, I'm afraid. How swift their ships:
Soaring, swooping. There's no more time.
Fear snakes my heart –
What use was headlong flight?
Father, I faint from fear.

DANAUS.
Courage. The Argive vote was firm.
They'll fight for you. I *know*.   740

CHORUS LEADER.
They are hawks, vultures,
Ravenous for war. This too you know.
They arrow the sea –
Dark hulls, a swarthy crew
Riding high on rage.

DANAUS.
>They'll find an army here, lean,
>In full summer-heat of strength.

CHORUS LEADER.
>Father, don't go. Don't abandon us.
>Women, alone – how can we fight?
>750 Harsh treachery they plan,
>Blasphemy; like carrion crows
>They'll plunder the altars of the gods.

DANAUS.
>It's to our advantage, children,
>If they disgust the gods.

CHORUS LEADER.
>If they scorn these altars, scorn the gods,
>How will they not lay hands on us?
>Rabid rage is theirs;
>Greed howls in them; they snarl
>And fear no god.

DANAUS.
>760 There's a saying: dogs cower to wolves.
>In Argos' cornfields no papyrus-seed shall grow.

CHORUS LEADER.
>They're like animals, unreason's cubs,
>Lust rules, not god. We must act against them *now*.

DANAUS.
>Be calm. The furling, the mooring of a fleet
>Takes time. Even with anchors safely dropped
>No prudent captain leaps to land
>At once, not on a harbourless shore
>At night when the sun has set.
>770 Night sharpens caution in experienced men.
>They'll not land their army till the ships
>Are snugly moored. There's time. Remember the gods
>And rule your fear, while I fetch help.
>Young words on old, wise lips: I'll make them come.

>*Exit.*

CHORUS.
    O earth, hills, justice of Argos,
    What will come of us? Where shall we go,
    In what dark pasture hide?
    Let us be smoke,
    Black smoke, like clouds,   780
    Like wingless dust,
    A puff of dust, invisible, away.

    Black terror bristles in our hearts;
    We tremble; our father's words take root;
    We're trapped; we flutter fear.
    Rather noose of death
    Than those hated hands
    Goosepimpling us;   790
    Rather death, and death's caress.

    Marry? And gnaw the heart?
    Sooner fall, sooner fall
    From sky-eyrie down,
    Snow-pillared in cloud,
    From brute rock down
    Scraping vulture-sky
    Where no goat leaps.
    Sooner fall! Sooner fall!

    A feast, a treasure-house   800
    For dogs and carrion birds.
    Fall to! Fall to!
    To die is to be free
    Of this misery, these tears.
    Come death! Come death!
    What other path,
    What bolt-hole from this marriage-bed?

    Shriek grief, howl prayers
    Till heaven hears, gods hear,
    Gods hear and help.   810
    Now! Now! Down! Down!
    Hear us. Help us. Look down on us,

Zeus, all-powerful, protector,
Who hates injustice,
Protect your suppliants.

Look on that rabble,
Aegyptus' sons:
Male lust, they pant,
820   They track us down,
Run as we may
They track us down.
Zeus, balance of the world,
It is in your hands!

Enter the EGYPTIAN CAPTAIN. *The* CHORUS
*breaks into incoherent cries, short o's and a's (as in the
words 'hot' and 'hat').*[31]

O! O! O! A! A! A!
Pirate. Rapist. Here.
Rapist. Drown!

CAPTAIN.
Come down. This way. Now.

CHORUS.
830   Pain. Hard pain begins.
Ee-ay. Ee-ay.
Run. Escape.
Violence. Hurting.
On land, on sea. Pain.
Earth-god, lord, protect!

CAPTAIN.
Quick. To ship.
Pick up your feet.
No? No?
Tearing, ripping,
840   Blood-pricks, necks chopped.
Hurry. Damn you. Get to the ship.

CHORUS.
Why didn't you drown
In your brass-pegged ship,

Choking arrogance
In roaring sea, salt sea?

CAPTAIN.
Ship, or suffer.
I order. No yowling,
Crazy hating.
Quick. Out of here.   850
Leave altars. Ship!
No place, no city.
I spit on you.

CHORUS.
Never see Nile again,
Soft water where cattle graze,
Pulse, flood of mortal life.
We're Argives. This is our land.

CAPTAIN.
You. Get to ship.   860
Willing or not. Quick.
We force. You go.
Struggling. Pain. Now.

CHORUS.
Aiee, aiee.
Struggle, die, drown.
Roaring sea,
Reefs, sand, lost,
Windblown, dead.

CAPTAIN.
Howl, shriek on gods.
You're caught. You'll not jump ship.
Howl, wail,   870
Make bitter, jagged. Shriek.

CHORUS.
O-ee, o-ee,
Rape, hissing jaws,
Crocodile, snatch, rape,
Bellow on land, on sea,

Nile, look Nile,
880 Flood, choke
Violence, choke rape.

CAPTAIN.
I order. Now. To ship.
Home-turning. Run.
Hair-dragging next: no mercy.

CHORUS.
O-ee. Father.
God-statues. Help. Betray.
Spider drags me,
Web, dream, black dream,
O-to-to-to-to-ee.
890 Ma. Gah. Ma. Gah.
Earth, mother, the snake,
I'm frightened, kill the snake,
O pa. Zeus. Earthson. Ah.

CAPTAIN.
Gods of this place – I'm not afraid.
They didn't suckle me, don't feed me now.

CHORUS.
It writhes near, two-legs, snake,
Viper, blood-fangs,
What name? What name?
Bite, savage pain,
O-toto-toto-ee.
900 Ma. Gah. Ma. Gah.
Earth, mother, the snake,
I'm frightened, kill the snake,
O pa. Zeus. Earthson. Ah.

CAPTAIN.
Hurry to the ship, now,
Or suffer fine clothes ripped. No mercy.

CHORUS.
Princes of Argos, help!

CAPTAIN.
Princes in Egypt soon you'll see:
You'll not go short of men.

CHORUS.
Lords of Argos, rape!

CAPTAIN.
Hair-tugging's next, it seems, dragging –
Unless you're sharp to hear my words.   910

Enter KING.[32]

KING.
You, what are you doing? Such arrogance!
You insult the men of Argos on their own soil.
Perhaps you think us women? We're Greeks:
No savage plays games with us.
Your arrows miss the mark; your plan misfires.

CAPTAIN.
I do nothing outside the law.

KING.
You're a stranger, a visitor: behave like one.

CAPTAIN.
I came for my own property. I take it; I go.

KING.
By what authority? Who speaks for you?

CAPTAIN.
Hermes the Searcher, who has priority.   920

KING.
You name our gods, but pay them no respect.

CAPTAIN.
Nile gods I worship, Egyptian gods.

KING.
And Argos' gods – do they mean nothing?

CAPTAIN.
I'll have these women. I'll not be robbed.

KING.
Touch them, and weep.

CAPTAIN.
A fine welcome you offer here.

KING.
 Not to those who plunder gods.

CAPTAIN.
 Shall I tell that to Aegyptus' sons?

KING.
 Do as you like. I'll not be moved.

CAPTAIN.
930 Who are you? I'm a messenger,
 I must be accurate, must tell it plain.
 Who are you who steals their property,
 Their cousins? The god of war will need
 No witnesses, no bribes, to try this case:
 Many will die, kick free of life, to settle it.

KING.
 Should I tell you my name? In time
 You'll learn it, you and your shipmates both.
 As for these women, you can take them –
940 If they agree, if the gods approve.
 If not, the city speaks with a single voice:
 We'll never give them up to force.
 Riveted firm this promise stands –
 Not scratched on tablets, locked in the folds of
     books,
 But firm and clear on free men's lips.
 Now, get out. Leave my sight. At once.

CAPTAIN.
950 War, war is being born.
 God bring heroes victory.

KING.
 Heroes? You'll find us heroes in Argos.
 No beerswillers here: we drink a stronger brew.

Exit CAPTAIN. *The* KING *addresses the* CHORUS.

Courage. Go with your maids
Inside the city walls, the ring of towers.
Secure, deep-rooted. We have houses there,

Lodgings, my own rich palace.
Choose where you like: to live
In a busy household, with others, 960
Or alone, if you prefer, in peace apart.
Choose what pleases best: it's yours.
I and all my citizens protect you now.
Vote given, vote obeyed. No other help you need.

CHORUS LEADER.
Lord King, for these good gifts
May good gifts teem in you.
Now, we beg you, send
Our father here, Danaus,
Rock, guide, counsellor. 970
His wisdom be our guide
What house, what place to choose.

Exit KING. *She addresses her sisters.*

We're strangers: the world's alert
For faults. May it find no fault in us!
Maidservants, take your places,
Each beside her mistress
As our father Danaus prescribed.[33]

Enter DANAUS.

DANAUS.
Children, to the people of Argos pray, 980
Sacrifice, make offerings: they're Olympian gods
To us, our saviours beyond all doubt.
I told them what we had suffered,
Their friends, their kin, at our cousins' hands;
They were sharp with anger, gave me soldiers,
Bodyguard of spears to mark my rank
And protect me from ambush, the hidden stroke of death
That would bring pollution, relentless, to choke this land.

990   For these kindnesses,
    Freighted with gratitude we must steer our course.
    To the store of my wisdom written in your hearts
    Add this: time is the touch-stone,
    The stranger's proving-ground. All people whisper
    At first against foreigners: easy slander, mud that
       sticks.
    Do nothing of desire to turn men's eyes.
    In a summer garden, when ripeness comes,
    Who can keep safe the fruit? Humans come,
1000   Animals, insect pests and birds –
    In gardens of desire, love spreads her feast.
    Pretty girls, unmarried, are a target
    Arrowed with lust by every passing eye.
    Remember, we travelled grievous seas,
    Seas of grief, to escape from this.
    Do nothing to bring me shame, joy to our enemies.
    Luck smiles: you've a choice of homes,
1010   With his Majesty, or housed at the city's cost.
    Cut chastity! Remember my words:
    Virginity's worth more that life itself.

CHORUS LEADER.
    Father, our luck's in the hands of God.
    As for our virginity, our summer fruit,
    Unless the gods send storms
    Our path is set, our minds are sure.

ARGIVE WOMEN *prepare to lead the*
DAUGHTERS *into the city in procession.*[34]

CHORUS.
    On! On! Radiant,
    Honour citylords,
1020   Happy gods, who cradle,
    Who haunt this land.
    Attendants, receive our song,
    For Argos our honouring.
    No longer for tumbling Nile;
    Rivers of Argos now
    We sing, who slip smooth,

Slip gentle across the land,
Life-pulse in veins of earth,
Virgin Artemis, smile on us,   1030
Keep rape at bay,
Love-wrestling, the little death.

WOMEN.
No! Sing Aphrodite; honour Love enthroned,
Whose power, with Hera's, stands next to Zeus.
Rainbow-tricks her skill,
Solemn acts her honouring.
Her children are soft Desire
And Persuasion, irresistible,   1040
Persuasion that skeins the heart.
In her procession Music plays,
Wanton fingers whisper love.

I'm afraid! Armadas of pain I see,
Fugitives, enemies, they step in blood.
They come, they skim the sea –
Why do winds smile on them?
What Fate decides, must be.
Zeus! Mindful, deep-purposing,
Your will, your will be done.
Marriage? Women's destiny: 1050
It's so, so it has always been.

CHORUS.
Great Zeus, protect!
No marriage with Aegyptus' sons!

WOMEN.
Pray only for the best.
You'll not charm fate.

CHORUS.
The future's not yours to know.
Who plumbs the mind of Zeus?
Who knows his purposes?

WOMEN.
Make him no demands.

CHORUS.

1060   What wisdom's this you teach?

WOMEN.

Make no demands on God.

CHORUS.

Zeus, lord, wither
Vile marriage threat,
Rape, whose healing hand
Held Io, whose gentle strength
Planted sturdy seed.
Allow us victory –
Women! Send what's best.

1070   Fate's dice are poised;
In Justice's name, for innocence,
Grant us this prayer.

Exeunt.

PROMETHEUS BOUND

Characters

PROMETHEUS
HEPHAESTUS
MIGHT
FORCE (silent part)
IO
OCEAN
HERMES
CHORUS OF OCEAN'S DAUGHTERS

Deserted mountainside. Enter HEPHAESTUS, MIGHT *and* FORCE, *with* PROMETHEUS *in chains*.[35]

MIGHT.

No further. This is Scythia. End of the world.
No exit. No tracks. No ... life.
Hephaestus, our father's orders: obey them now.
Spike that criminal, here on these crags.
Iron pegs, steel chains. No breaking.
Your flower he stole, your fire,
Spark of all knowledge. To give to mortals!
That was his crime. His punishment: whatever
The gods demand. He must turn his face
From mortals, and learn to love lord Zeus.   10

HEPHAESTUS.

Might, Force, you *are* the word of Zeus.
He orders; you obey; you are fulfilled.
But I – how can I bring myself
To bind a kinsman here in this wintry place?
I must. To ignore Zeus' word is no careless thing.
Prometheus, noble-hearted son
Of Themis the counsellor,
Not I, not you, chose this.
I'll spike you here on this hill.   20
No mortals to hear, to see. Sun's rays
Will scorch you, wither you. You'll cry
For starry-mantled Night to douse the fire –
And cry again, when next day's Sun
Scatters the dew and renews your pain.
Forever. No blunting the tooth of pain.
Your rescuer's unborn, does not exist.
You chose it. Mortal-lover! Chose it yourself.
A god, you laughed at gods. You gave
What was theirs to mortals. Free choice!   30
Now brood on that, here on this rock.
No rest. No sleep. Limbs locked with cramp.
You'll groan. You'll curse. You'll shriek.
You'll not move Zeus. All new-throned kings are harsh.

MIGHT.

Time-wasting! Weeping! All in vain.
Why love the god all gods detest?

He gave your pride to mortals.

HEPHAESTUS.
But kinship … fellowship …

MIGHT.
40   Zeus speaks, and you ignore.
Do you dare? Are you not afraid?

HEPHAESTUS.
You're made of stone. No pity.

MIGHT.
For him? Sing dirges? Save your breath.
You've work to do.

HEPHAESTUS.
I curse my skill –

MIGHT.
Why? Bluntly,
Did your skill bring him here?

HEPHAESTUS.
Perhaps someone else –

MIGHT.
Who? All are slaves, feel pain.
50   All creation. Only Zeus is free.

HEPHAESTUS.
How can I argue?

MIGHT.
Hurry, then. Chain him,
Before Zeus spots you hesitating.

HEPHAESTUS.
The manacles are here.

MIGHT.
Round his wrists. Hammer. Hard!
Peg him to the rock.

HEPHAESTUS.
No hesitation now.

MIGHT.
>Harder. Wedge tighter.
>He'll snatch any chance to wriggle free.

HEPHAESTUS.
>He'll not work this arm loose.   60

MIGHT.
>The other one. Hit hard! He's clever:
>Teach him Zeus is cleverer.

HEPHAESTUS.
>It's done. Only he could blame me now.

MIGHT.
>Spike him. Beak of steel drives
>Through flesh and bone and bites the rock.

HEPHAESTUS.
>Prometheus, I weep for your pain –

MIGHT.
>Still crying for Zeus' enemies?
>Be careful. You may be next.

HEPHAESTUS.
>You see a sight that tears the eye –

MIGHT.
>A criminal getting what he's earned.   70
>Tight round his ribs.

HEPHAESTUS.
>I know my orders. Save your breath.

MIGHT.
>I'll tell you in detail, exactly what to do.
>Go lower. Hoop his legs. Hit hard.

HEPHAESTUS.
>It's done. It was easy: look.

MIGHT.
>Tighter. Hammer harder. The foreman
>Who'll inspect this work is hard.

HEPHAESTUS.
>You're hard, too. Looks, voice ... hard.

MIGHT.
>*You* be soft. I don't give way.
>I'm what I am. I'm not to blame.

80

HEPHAESTUS.
>It's done. He's chained. Let's go.

MIGHT (*to* PROMETHEUS).
>There. Now defy the gods. Plunder,
>Squander their gifts on mortals.
>Will mortals ease this pain?
>Prometheus, 'Farsighted'. What a name!
>Be farsighted now. See how
>To wriggle out of this!

Exeunt MIGHT, FORCE *and* HEPHAESTUS.

PROMETHEUS.
>Day-brightness, winds on beating wings,
>Rivers, waves of the myriad-laughing sea,
>Earth mother of all, bright Sun,
>See me, a god.
>See how gods treat god.
>See my agony:
>I must wrestle eternity,
>Gnawed by this pain.
>His doing! The new one,
>Tyrant of the blessed –
>See what he found for me.
>A-ah! A-ah! Pain now,
>Pain then, unending pain.
>I weep for them.

90

100

>What end will he ordain for them?
>Far-sighted! I know them all.
>No stranger-pain will come.
>This is my fate, and I must bear it.
>No struggling. Destiny:
>What power can master it?
>Shall I tell my fate? Not tell?

Both hard. I gave a gift
To mortals, and in that giving
Yoked myself to fate – to this!
I filled a hollow reed with fire,
Stolen from heaven. I gave it
To mortals. It sparked them,
Taught them cunning, filled their need.   110
For that, now, I pay this price,
Chained, staked, wide open to the sky.

Ah! E-ah!
Sound. Smell. No words.
God-sent? Mortal? Demigod?
Has it come to creation's edge
To gape? What would it see?
A god in chains, accursed,
The enemy of Zeus, despised   120
By all who throng his court.
Prometheus, mortal-lover. Here I am!

Birds. I hear a flock of birds.
Wings whisper in the air.
Whatever is coming, I fear it.

Enter the CHORUS *of* OCEAN'S DAUGHTERS.[36]

CHORUS.
Fear nothing. We are your friends.
Swift wing-beats bring friends,
Here to this cliff   130
On the chariot of the winds.
From our sea-cave far below
We heard iron ring on iron.
At once, barefoot –
No meek-eyed modesty –
We mounted our chariot of wings
To weep with you.

PROMETHEUS.
A-ah! A-ah!
Daughters of fertile Tethys

140   And of Ocean whose tides
    Unsleeping gird the Earth,
    Look, see me nailed,
    Chained, here
    On the eyebrow of this hilltop,
    Keeping watch,
    A vigil no one envies.

CHORUS.
    We see you, Prometheus.
    Our eyes blur with tears,
    With fear, to see you
    Chained to this rock.
    A new pilot steers Olympus:
150   Young king, young laws,
    No precedent.
    The glory of the past,
    The might of yesterday –
    Who remembers them?

PROMETHEUS.
    If he'd hurled me down,
    To Tartarus beyond escape,
    Chained me there
    Far below Hades' kingdom of corpses,
    I'd have borne it.
    Who'd have mocked me then? Which god?
    Which … other? Instead, look!, I hang here,
    The wind's plaything,
    Joy to my enemies.

CHORUS.
160   Which enemies? Which gods
    Are so rock-hearted as to laugh?
    Who finds no tears
    To echo such suffering? None but Zeus.
    He'll not bend. He'll break
    The children of Sky, not rest
    Till he gluts his heart
    Or someone comes with tricks
    To snatch that throne of his.

PROMETHEUS.
>My time will come. Racked, enfettered,
>Still I know this: his lordship,
>Immortal king, will send for me
>To tell him the secret I know,   170
>The plan to snatch his power, his rank.
>When that day comes, he can fawn on me,
>Honey my ears with soft persuasion,
>Threaten me faint with fear;
>I'll still keep silent. Let him crawl;
>Let him break these chains, pay recompense
>For all my suffering. Then I'll speak.

CHORUS.
>Brave words. Your spirit chafes
>At suffering, and will not yield.
>But you go too far.   180
>Fear arrows my heart.
>You drift in a sea of pain –
>What harbour, then, is set for you?
>Zeus, Kronos' son, is harsh.
>He'll not be persuaded.

PROMETHEUS.
>His highness thinks
>That justice is his alone.
>But one day he'll melt:
>Ice-heart will thaw,   190
>He'll run to me, smile for smile,
>With friendship in his hands.

CHORUS LEADER.
>What caused his anger? Tell us.
>What crime deserved such punishment,
>Such injustice? Tell us,
>Unless telling, too, is dangerous.

PROMETHEUS.
>If I speak, I suffer. Silence, too, brings pain.
>All's misery. No escape.

When civil war began in Olympus,
200   Two factions split the gods. Some chose
To topple Kronos, snatch his throne for Zeus.
The rest were hot that Zeus should never rule.
I went to the Titans, children of Earth and Sky,
Offered them strategy. They laughed me down;
Their muscles promised strength would win.
I said, 'Our mother – Themis, Earth,
She has many names –
210   Foretold the future.
Fate's decree. Not strength
But guile will win.'
Deaf ears; they turned away.
I took my mother's words to Zeus. My gift,
Freely given freely taken. By my plan
Tartarus' deeps enfold the Titans,
220   Kronos and all his army. Zeus is king,
By my plans – and pays me with these pains.
All tyrants are galled by the same disease:
They dare not trust their friends.

But you asked my guilt, what crime deserved
This agony. I'll tell you.
He was not yet warm on his father's throne
When he began rewarding his acolytes,
230   Granting each god new powers, new privilege.
Humans he ignored. No word, just loathing.
Stamp them out and start again.
In all Olympus only I said no. I dared.
I held off the thunderbolt, saved the human race
From Hades' halls – and for that he spiked me here,
Tormented, racked, an abject sight to see.
240   I pitied humans; who now pities me?
This punishment, this agony, dishonours Zeus.

CHORUS LEADER.
Iron-hearted, carved from stone, Prometheus,
Are those who see your suffering, and find
No tears to shed. Unwilling witnesses,
We see you now. Your anguish wrings our hearts.

PROMETHEUS.
Friends at least can look on me, and pity.

CHORUS LEADER.
Was there more guilt? Is there more to tell?

PROMETHEUS.
My mortals feared the future. I ended that.

CHORUS LEADER.
What cure did you find for that disease?

PROMETHEUS.
Hope, planted in their hearts. Blind hope.   250

CHORUS LEADER.
A generous gift for creatures born to die.

PROMETHEUS.
One other thing I gave them: fire.

CHORUS LEADER.
The creatures of a day have fire? Bright fire?

PROMETHEUS.
And with it knowledge: yes.

CHORUS LEADER.
And for this crime lord Zeus –

PROMETHEUS.
Torments me and will never set me free.

CHORUS LEADER.
No end is fixed?

PROMETHEUS.
Until he chooses, none.

CHORUS LEADER.
Why should he choose? How can you hope for that?
Can't you see your sin? What other name   260
Can I give it, sweeter to say, to hear?
Think up some way to escape your pain.

PROMETHEUS.
It's easy to gush with good advice

From outside the snare. 'You're trapped. Do this.
   Do that.'
I knew what would happen, from the start.
I chose. I chose. I'll not deny it.
By helping mortals, I condemned myself.
But how could I foresee such punishment?
Chained to this giddy rock,
270   Alone in this wilderness, left to rot?
Don't waste your tears on the suffering you see.
Come closer ... step down ... and hear the rest,
The future. Do as I ask. Do as I ask.
Share my sorrow. Pain's a restless wanderer,
Settles now here, now there.

CHORUS LEADER.
    Prometheus, we hear and answer.
    Light-footed – look! –
    We step from chariot,
280   Step down from Sky,
    Stand here on stony ground.
    Tell all your grief:
    We're listening.
    Enter OCEAN.[37]

OCEAN.
    Prometheus, I've travelled fast and far
    To see you, beyond the boundaries.
    My steed needed no bit, no bridle:
    My will sufficed to guide him.
    I weep for what has happened.
290   Kin-duty – and more than that,
    Warm friendship. We need
    No flattery, you and I:
    Tell me the help you want,
    It's yours. You'll never say
    You've a truer friend than Ocean.

PROMETHEUS.
    Ocean! Have you too come to gape?
    Have you brought yourself to leave
300   The waters called after you, the caves

Self-hollowed? Here, to this iron land,
To drink my misery, to weep for me?
Look, then. I was Zeus' friend,
I set him up in power;
This rack is my reward.

OCEAN.
I see, Prometheus, and I offer good advice –
Hear it, for all your cleverness.
Know yourself. New ways: accept them.
A new king rules the immortals.   310
Fling bitter words, sharp as knives,
He'll hear, for all his throne is far away,
And your present throng of pain
Will seem like a children's game.
Poor friend, control your anger,
Look for a way to earn release.
Old advice, but still the best.
You were proud before, Prometheus.
Words vaulted from your tongue,
Earned you this – and still you refuse   320
To bend, pile pain on pain. Listen.
Learn from me. Don't kick the goad.
Our ruler's hard, does as he likes,
Accountable to none. Let me go to him,
Work on him to free you.
Meantime, bite your tongue, lie quiet –
Or is the only thing you've never learned
That foolish talk earns sharpest pain?

PROMETHEUS.
So lucky! To share with me, to dare,   330
And still stand free of punishment!
Stay clear. Don't meddle. He won't
Be wooed; you'll not persuade him.
Look out for yourself. There's danger here.

OCEAN.
Always good advice for others,
None for yourself! I take my cue
From what you do, not what you say.
My decision's made. Don't stop me.

I know, I know lord Zeus will grant
The favour I ask: to set you free.

PROMETHEUS.

340   Such loyalty! Such eagerness!
I'm grateful. But give up now.
You'll fail. You'll put yourself out, and fail.
Do nothing. Stay away from it.
How will it help my suffering
To share it with all my friends?
I weep for my brother-Titans: Atlas,
Far in the west, who bears

350   The pillar of the universe, a weight to strain
      endurance.
Hundred-headed Typhon,[38] who left his lair
In the caverns of Cilicia to topple Zeus.
His jaws hissed terror. His eyes
Flashed gorgon-glances. Still he fell.
Zeus' thunderbolt, unsleeping fire,

360   Blasted his boasting, scorched his strength.
Witless now, shapeless, limp,
He lies by the narrow sea,
Pinned under Etna, while on the peak above
Hephaestus perches, smithying.
One day rivers of fire will gush from there,
Gulping green Sicily,

370   As Typhon vomits rage, torrents of rock
Spewed, red-hot, from thunder-ash.
Why do I tell you this? You know it.
Save yourself. I'll bear my fate,
Endure it to the end – till Zeus relents.

OCEAN.

Can't you understand, Prometheus?
Soft words are anger's antidote.

PROMETHEUS.

If the time is right, if the heart is soft.

380   If not, they rub it raw.

OCEAN.

You say I'm over-hasty.
What harm in that?

PROMETHEUS.
    Wasted labour … fatuous –

OCEAN.
    Let me be fatuous, then. A healthy sickness,
    To mask good sense in foolishness.

PROMETHEUS.
    I'd be foolish to let you try.

OCEAN.
    Your advice is clear: 'Go home' –

PROMETHEUS.
    Or you'll earn hatred too.

OCEAN.
    From his new high lordship?

PROMETHEUS.
    Watch out for him. Do nothing to rouse his rage.   390

OCEAN.
    Your suffering, Prometheus, teaches that.

PROMETHEUS.
    Go, then. Before you change your mind.

OCEAN.
    Your words find no deaf ears.
    Already my steed is fretting the sky
    With eager wings. He longs to settle
    And relax in his own familiar stall.

    Exit.

CHORUS.
    We cry your fate, Prometheus,
    Your bitter fate.
    Gentle eyes well tears;
    Rivulets
    Stain soft cheeks.   400
    Oppression. Tyranny.
    Zeus hardens his heart,
    Makes laws unchallenged
    To trample powers of old.

Earth cries your fate, Prometheus,
Cries out your fate.
Powers, principalities,
410 Long-honoured,
Weep for you now.
Mortals of Asia, proud
In ancient land, groan
With your groaning,
Pine with your pain.

In Colchis, Amazons
Who fear no fight.
In Scythia, hordes
By the waters of Lake Maeotis,
Brink of the world.

420 In Arabia, the flower
Of warriors,
High in the hills,
By Caucasus, baying for battle,
Bristling spears.

One other, one only,
Is yoked to such punishment:
Atlas, straining age-old strength
To heft the whole world's weight
430 And sky above.

Waves roll on empty sea,
Furl, crash, roar. Groan for you
Chasms, caverns, the gulf of hell.
Quicksilver water-springs
Weep bitter tears.

PROMETHEUS.
Stiff-necked you think me? Too proud to speak?
Not so. Shame gnaws my heart,
Rage at the outrage done to me.
It was I – you know it – I and no other

Who handed these gods their power. No more   440
Of that. But hear how it was with mortals.
Blank minds. I planted seeds of thought,
Intelligence. No shame to them in this:
I tell it to show how good my gift.
They had eyes but saw nothing, ears
But could not hear. Like dream-people
They blundered from birth to death.
They built no houses, from brick or wood: 450
Termites, they scrabbled underground
In runs and hollows, sunless.
They knew no seasons – winter, flowery spring,
Abundant summer passed them by.

Life without reason. Then I helped them.
I showed them the stars' elusive movements,
Rising and setting. I taught them numbers,
Skill of skills, and writing,
All-memory, mother of arts.   460
I tamed wild animals, yoked them
To drudge for mortals. Horses I broke
And harnessed, trained to draw
The glittering chariots the wealthy love.
I gave them ships, sail-carts
With wings to ride the sea.
These were my gifts to mortals –   470
Who now can find no cleverness to help myself.

CHORUS LEADER.
  Heart's grief. Mind-sick.
  You're rudderless,
  A sickly doctor
  Who dare not dose himself.

PROMETHEUS.
  Apt words, when you hear the rest,
  The other skills and ways I found for them.
  Greatest of all: when they fell ill
  They had no remedy. No drugs,
  No ointments. They withered and died,   480
  Until I taught them to mix soothing herbs,

Defence against all disease.
I showed them the paths of prophecy:
How to unravel dreams and oracles,
Interpret meetings on a journey,
Read the flight of hook-toed birds –
490   The luck each movement meant, each cry,
When they flocked or fought.
Secrets of sacrifice I showed them: the gloss
Of entrails, what colour pleased the gods,
Delicate spectrum of liver and heart.
I taught them to wrap thighs in fat, to burn
The long shank-bone, what signs to seek
In smoky altar-fires. I dazzled them
With star-patterns, before unknown.
What more? Who found for them
500   Wealth hidden in the ground: iron, copper, gold?
I did: admit it, all who believe in truth.
It's briefly told: whatever mortals know
They learned from me –

CHORUS LEADER.
You gave them everything.
You've nothing left to give yourself.
But still we hope.
One day you'll be free.
510   You'll rival Zeus.

PROMETHEUS.
Not yet. Ten thousand agonies
I must endure, then break these chains.
There's no escape:
Necessity outmatches skill.

CHORUS LEADER.
Who steers Necessity?

PROMETHEUS.
The trinity of Fates, the watchful Furies.

CHORUS LEADER.
They outmatch even Zeus?

PROMETHEUS.
Even Zeus is prisoner to Fate.

CHORUS LEADER.
    What is his fate? Eternal rule?

PROMETHEUS.
    Don't ask. That secret stays.   520

CHORUS LEADER.
    A dreadful secret, if you hide it so!

PROMETHEUS.
    Ask something else. I'll not tell that.
    Not yet. I'll hide it, clutch it close –
    My secret, the knowledge I hold
    To smash these chains and set me free.

CHORUS.
    May Zeus all-powerful never
    Set his might against my will.
    May I untiring pay the gods
    Due sacrifice, hecatombs   530
    By Ocean's unfailing stream,
    Never sin in words.
    Precepts fixed for me, pillars
    Beyond erosion.

    Sweet, sweet, to fatten long life on hope,
    Banquets of joy, soul-feasts.
    I see you ragged-raw,   540
    Ten thousand pains,
    See you and shudder.
    Prometheus, free spirit,
    You championed mortals,
    Refused to cringe to Zeus.

    You gave – what recompense?
    What help from them? Strengthless,
    Creatures of a day, dream-beings
    Impotent, blind, death-bound.
    How could such puniness –
    Why could you not see? –
    Ever smudge the pattern, tear   550
    The web of Zeus' law?

This song today, Prometheus,
Pain-song, tear-song,
Flies from our lips,
Not like that other song we sang,
Wedding-song, bath-song, bed-song,
When you wooed Hesione,[39]
Your fellow-Titan, took her
560   For consort, bedmate, queen.

Enter IO.[40]

IO.
What land? What people? Who
Fettered here to rock,
Enduring?
What guilt? Such punishment!
Tell, where
Pain drags me, here on Earth.

A! A! E! E!
Stings, again, gadfly,
Spectre of earthborn Argus.
Alyoo, Ah Dah! I fear him,
The shepherd, the thousand eyes.
570   Crafty-looker, stalker, dead,
Sprouted again from Earth,
From inner gulfs, hunting-dog
Yapping me down lonely, hungry shore.

Reedpipe drowses:
Lullabies, cicada-songs.
A-ah! A-ah! Where
Am I wandering, wandering, ah?
Zeus son of Kronos, why, what guilt
Yokes me to this pain?
E! E!
580   Gadfly, sting, afraid,
Worn witless, why?
Cinder me, smother me,
Bait me for sharks,
I pray, I pray,
O hear me, lord.

Wandering, wandering,
Learning, but still no way
To end this pain.
Lows the cow-horned maid. D'you hear? D'you hear?

PROMETHEUS.
Io's voice: Io, daughter of Inachus,
Whose love flamed Zeus' heart.   590
Now, gadfly-stung, she lopes the world
Endlessly, hopelessly, nagged by Hera's hate.

IO.
Io, daughter of Inachus. You say my name.
Speak to my wretchedness.
Who are you? How do you know   600
My punishment, God's plague,
How it stings, it goads, it gnaws?
E! E!
Bounding, loping, starving
I pelted here,
Twisted by Hera's rage,
Her jealous rage.
Who, E! E!,
In all creation's agony
Has ever known pain like mine?
Tell me, true,
What suffering more? What cure,
What medicine to end this pain?
If you know it, speak.
Asks the wanderer, the sufferer. Speak, oh speak!

PROMETHEUS.
I'll tell you. All.
No riddles. A friend's duty,   610
To open the mouth to friends.
You see Prometheus, who handed mortals fire.

IO.
Prometheus – ah! Beacon of blessing you shone
For creatures of day. Why this reward?

PROMETHEUS.
I've told my tale of tears.

IO.
> But not to me. I beg you, grant me –

PROMETHEUS.
> Ask.

IO.
> Who punished you? Who nailed you here?

PROMETHEUS.
> Lord Zeus' orders. Hephaestus' hands.

IO.
620   What crime earned such a punishment?

PROMETHEUS.
> The one I told you. Nothing more.

IO.
> One other thing. Tell me:
> The length, the limit of my wandering.

PROMETHEUS.
> Better not to know –

IO.
> Don't hide my agony.

PROMETHEUS.
> I don't begrudge you.

IO.
> What, then? Tell!

PROMETHEUS.
> I hesitate to hurt.

IO.
> You spare me more than I spare myself.

PROMETHEUS.
630   If you insist, I'll speak.

CHORUS LEADER.
> Not yet. Grant us a favour too!
> First let her tell what caused

Her sickness, her wandering.
Then you reveal the suffering still in store.

PROMETHEUS.
Tell them, Io. Ocean's daughters,
Your father's sisters!
Tell them: shared grief,
A tale of tears well told
To willing ears, is easier to bear.

IO.
Should I trust you? Distrust you? Hear   640
The tale you asked for, briefly told.
And yet ... god-storms, disfigured innocence.
I blush to speak.

Night-phantoms jostled round my maiden bed
And whispered,
'Why still virgin?
Lucky girl, who could give yourself to power.
Zeus burns to sleep with you.
To sleep with you – lord Zeus!   650
Don't spurn him. Go to Lerna,
Where sheep and cattle browse
In your father's grassy meadows.
Ease Zeus there.'
The same dream, night after night, tormented me.
At last, in desperation, I told my father,
And he sent messengers to Delphi and Dodona
To ask what he should do or say to placate   660
The gods. They brought back riddles,
A tangle of oracles and prophecies,
Impossible to unravel. Then at last,
Like a piercing ray of light, Apollo spoke
Clearly and simply. I was to be banished,
To roam the fringes of creation,
Exiled from all I loved. If my father refused,
God's fire-faced thunderbolt would kill us all.
Apollo's oracle. My father wept; I wept;   670
But Zeus' goad bites deep.
I went. They slammed the gates behind me.

Looks and mind contorted,
Horned as you see me,
Gadfly-stung, I bucked and ran
By Cerchneia, sweet to drink,
By Lerna's spring.
Argus, Earthborn, herded me:
Rage, a thousand eyes, tracking, tracking ...
680 Fate stole his life, when least he looked for it,
Leaving me, god-scourged, the gadfly,
Goaded, ends of the Earth. O Prometheus,
If you know what else I must suffer,
I beg you, tell me now. Don't pity me,
Don't comfort me with lies:
False words are germs. They breed, they kill.

CHORUS.
Ah! Stop! Ee-ah!
690 Unheard-of! Hear, see, shudder.
Agony. Stab, goad,
Soul-freeze. Yoh! Yoh! Fate.
We hear, and cringe.

PROMETHEUS.
Too soon. These wails, these shudders.
Save tears till you hear the rest.

CHORUS LEADER.
Speak, tell. It soothes to know
How long the pain, what suffering remains.

PROMETHEUS.
700 Your first prayer I granted:
To hear her tell how suffering began.
Now hear the rest: pain planned for her,
Ordained by Hera.
Io, daughter of Inachus,
Store my words, hear your journey to the end.
Turn first to the rising Sun.
Tread empty sand.
You'll see nomads, Scythians who live
710 In wicker houses built on ox-carts:
Archers, whose arrows kill from far.

Avoid them.
Keep to the coast that hems their country.
Surf, wave-roar.
On your left, iron-working Chalybes.
Savages, harsh with strangers. Pass them by.
Hybristes next. Insolence: a river aptly named.
If you try to cross, you'll drown.
Follow it instead:
Up, up, where it spurts from highest peaks
On Caucasus, ceiling of the world. Climb here,   720
Rock-pinnacles beside the stars, then down,
South, where Amazons live, women warriors
Who scorn all men, whose home one day will be
Themiscyra, round Thermodon, beside
Salmydessus, cursed by sailors,
Ship-swallower, whose rocks bite sea.
Guides, Amazons, will take you to Cimmeria,
The isthmus, the gateway. Glad-hearted,   730
Pass over, cross the seaway. Ever after,
Mortals will call it after you:
Cow-crossing, Bosphorus.
Out of Europe, into Asia.

To the CHORUS.

You see his arrogance, the gods' new king?
All crushed alike. He lusted for her, god
For mortal, dizzied her with wandering.
A harsh seducer, Io. All I've said   740
Is hardly the beginning of your pain.

IO (*lowing and bucking*).
   Yoh! Mah! E! E!

PROMETHEUS.
   Yes, moan, low, cry. What will you do
   When I tell you the suffering still to come?

CHORUS LEADER.
   There's more? More suffering still to tell?

PROMETHEUS.
   A sea. A storm.

IO.
> Why do I go on living? I could climb
> To the lip of the precipice, dash myself down
> And be quit of all my troubles.
750 > Better once to die
> Than to drag out each day in misery.

PROMETHEUS.
> And what of me?
> How would you bear my pain?
> Immortal: no death-hopes comfort me.
> No end to misery, so long as Zeus is king.

IO.
> So long – ? His power will end?

PROMETHEUS.
> You'd smile to see it?

IO.
> He tortures me!

PROMETHEUS.
760 > His power will end.

IO.
> Who'll end it?

PROMETHEUS.
> Himself. His brainless majesty.

IO.
> How? Tell, if tell you can.

PROMETHEUS.
> He'll make ... a union.

IO.
> With god? With mortal? Speak!

PROMETHEUS.
> That answer is forbidden.

IO.
> His ... partner will take his throne?

PROMETHEUS.
She'll bear a son, mightier than his father.

IO.
Has he no way to save himself?

PROMETHEUS.
Only my release.   770

IO.
Who'll free you? Zeus forbids it.

PROMETHEUS.
A descendant of yours, the Fates decree.[41]

IO.
My descendant will set you free?

PROMETHEUS.
Three generations, three and ten.

IO.
A riddling prophecy. Unguessable.

PROMETHEUS.
Then ask no more about yourself.

IO.
You offer favours, then snatch them back.

PROMETHEUS.
Two stories. I'll tell you one of them.

IO.
Which? Tell me. Let me choose.

PROMETHEUS.
Your sufferings, every detail still to come,   780
Or who it is who'll set me free. Now choose.

CHORUS LEADER.
Two stories, one for her and one for us.
Tell her her wanderings, us your saviour's name.
A favour: grant it. We long to hear.

PROMETHEUS.
Since you're so eager, I agree. I'll tell.

First, Io. Your tearful wanderings:
Write them in your mind.

790   You'll cross the sea that divides the continents,
Tread deserts scorched by Sun's bright eye,
Along booming shore to Cisthene's plains
Where monsters live. Phorcys' daughters,
Swan-women old as the stars.
One eye they share, one tooth.
Their like no sun, no moon, has seen.
Not far away their sisters: Gorgons,
Winged, snake-haired, implacable.

800   No mortal looks on them and lives:
I tell you this for your own protection.
There are fiercer guardians to hear of:
Wolf-vultures, Zeus' hunting-pack,
Beaked, fanged, silent; one-eyed Arimaspians,
Horse-warriors, who live where Pluto's stream,
Gold-laden, bubbles from the ground. Avoid them.
On to a distant land, black people, who live
By the river Aethiops, birth-spring of the Sun.

810   Follow it as far as the mountains of Biblus,
The waterfall where holy Nile is born.
Its waters, pure to drink, will lead you
To the Delta, distant home decreed by Fate
For you and your descendants forever.
Io, your future. If there are riddles left,
Ask. I'll explain. Time hangs on my hands.

CHORUS LEADER.
If she has more weary wandering to hear,
820   Tell her. If you've told them all, remember
And grant that favour you promised us.

PROMETHEUS.
I've told her all her wandering. Its end.
To prove, now, that what I say is true,
No invention, I'll tell what she endured
Before she came here. A crowded tale. I choose
The last stage only, these last days.
You came to the plains of Molossus, Io,

To Dodona, Zeus' shrine, where talking trees   830
Miraculously utter oracles.
Clearly, no riddles,
The voices greeted you: 'Hail, majesty,
Consort of Zeus that shall be'.
Do you smile at that?
Next, gadfly-goaded, down to the coast,
To the Gulf of Rhea. Storms drove you back,
But that sea will bear your name: Ionian,   840
Reminding mortals forever of your wandering.
I tell you this to prove how I can see
Further and deeper than is revealed.

To the CHORUS.

The rest I tell to you and her together.
I pick up the tale where I broke it off before.
In Canopus, settlement at creation's edge,
The Delta, where Nile pours silt to clog the sea:
There Zeus will come to you, restore your wits –
Tenderly, gently, touch that brings no fear.   850
You'll bear a dark-skinned son: Apis, bull-king,
Who'll reap wherever Nile waters fertile soil.
His descendant Danaus, in the fifth generation,
Will fly with fifty daughters from there
To Argos, saving them from rape
By their own cousins. Hot for them,
Hawks for doves, the cousins will swoop.
Forbidden prey: the gods will cheat them.
Argive earth will swallow them,   860
Deathstruck, outwomaned, murder in the dark.
Each daughter's blade will run with one man's life –
If only my enemies could find such love!
One man, one only, will be saved.
His girl will smile on him as he sleeps.
Desire will blunt her purpose, stay her hand.
She'll choose
To be called coward not murderer;
Her descendants, dynasty of kings,
Will rule in Argos. To cut it short,   870
A hero, a famous archer, born of her line,

Will set me free. This is my future, Io,
Foretold by Themis, Mother Earth
As old as time. But how it will happen, when –
Too long to tell, no profit to you to know.

IO.
Eleleu! Eleleu!
Madness! Brain bubbles, burns.
880   Gadfly goads, sharp steel
Forged in no fire.
Heart bucks for fear,
Eyes roll. Mist,
Whirlwind, driven.
Tongue raves,
Words jostle, spate,
River of madness, storm of fate.

Exit.

CHORUS.
Wise, wise who first
Established, first proclaimed this law:
890   Seek no relationship above yourself.
Let not those who work with hands aspire
To marry into families
Flaunting wealth or ancestry.

Never, never see
Us, long-lived Muses, share Zeus' bed,
Unite with lover from the stars.
Io's fate we see, and shudder:
900   Virgin blighted by Hera,
Ravaged unravaged, wandering.

Marriage equal-matched,
No threat. Fasten
No god's hot eye on us. Fight no-fight,
Love no-love; we fear it.
What could we do?
Zeus raging – how escape?

PROMETHEUS.
Almighty Zeus! Stiff-necked and obstinate,

Still he'll fall one day. The match he's planning
Will topple him from power forever.   910
As his father Kronos was driven into exile
He cursed his son – and that curse lives on,
And will soon be carried out. Only I
Of all immortals, only I can tell him
How to escape destruction. Let him rule!
Let him perch on his throne, hug thunderbolts!
Not even they will save him, shield him
Against disaster, dishonour, a fall
Beyond endurance. His adversary – monstrous,   920
Unstoppable – will outface his lightning,
Deafen his thunder, smash Poseidon's spear
That shakes the land, stirs up the sea.
Zeus will trip and fall, and in his falling learn
The gulf between ruling and being ruled.

CHORUS LEADER.
  These are wishes, not threats, to hurl at Zeus.

PROMETHEUS.
  His fate, my wishes. All will be fulfilled.

CHORUS LEADER.
  You say a power will arise, and outmatch Zeus?   930

PROMETHEUS.
  Will give him grief more than I suffer now.

CHORUS LEADER.
  You dare him with words. You should be afraid.

PROMETHEUS.
  Of what? An immortal – what have I to fear?

CHORUS LEADER.
  He'll send you sharper grief than death.

PROMETHEUS.
  He'll not surprise me.

CHORUS LEADER.
  Wiser to bow to fate, accept necessity.

PROMETHEUS.
  You grovel! Kiss dust at Zeus' feet.

He's less than that dust to me.
He has a little moment of ruling left:

940   Let him enjoy it! He won't rule heaven long.
Oh look. His page-boy,
His jumped-up majesty's step-and-fetch.
What fearful message is he bringing us?

Enter HERMES.

HERMES.
Word-spinner, insult-monger,
Who pedestalled mortals above the gods,
Fire-thief, hear me. Our father's orders:
This marriage you boast will topple him.
Name it, now. No riddles. Tell everything.

950   Prometheus, I'll not come twice.
Chains, spikes, pain –
Hard proof that Zeus is not to be talked down.

PROMETHEUS.
Big threats, big boasting. Lapdog of the gods!
New gods, new powers.
You think sky-battlements beyond all threats.
But so did Kronos, once.
I've seen two tyrants fall; I'll see a third,
Fastest and farthest. What, must I flatter,

960   Fawn on that upstart? Run away. Run home.
Your journey's wasted. Answer is refused.

HERMES.
We've heard such insolence before.
It berthed you here. Self-chosen agony.

PROMETHEUS.
I look at this. I look at you.
Torment or slavery? I wouldn't change.

HERMES.
You'd change. What? Slave to this rock,
Or personal messenger to father Zeus?

PROMETHEUS.
    Upstart for upstart. Pleased with yourself?   970

HERMES.
    Aren't you? Taking pride in pain.

PROMETHEUS.
    I long to see one day
    My enemies so proud, so gratified. You.

HERMES.
    You blame me too?

PROMETHEUS.
    All gods. I hate them all.
    I put them where they are. They put me here.

HERMES.
    You're sick. Deranged. No cure.

PROMETHEUS.
    It's sick to hate my enemies? I'm sick.

HERMES.
    If you were well, how would we cope with you?

PROMETHEUS (a cry of pain).
    Aaah!

HERMES.
    Cry on. But remember: Zeus is deaf.   980

PROMETHEUS.
    Time passing will unstop his ears.

HERMES.
    Time passing. Was it that made you so wise?

PROMETHEUS.
    How, wise, and squander words on crawlers?

HERMES.
    You'll tell our father nothing?

PROMETHEUS.
    In spite of all his kindness –

HERMES.
> You treat me like a child.

PROMETHEUS.
> You are a child, a babe in arms,
> If you expect an answer. Nothing –
> No rack, no ... instrument devised by Zeus
990   Will make me speak. Until he sets me free.
> Whirlwinds of fire, ice-storms, thunder-roars
> To engulf the Earth. Hurl! Churn! Destroy!
> Let him do what he likes. Until I choose
> He'll not know who it is who'll topple him.

HERMES.
> Think, Prometheus. What will you gain by this?

PROMETHEUS.
> I've all eternity to think.

HERMES.
> Fool! Learn from this pain,
1000   Change your mind while still there's time.

PROMETHEUS.
> Lecture the tides. You'll not change me.
> What? Whimper to the one I hate,
> Wheedle, palms upwards,
> Like a woman,
> Till he slips these chains?
> I'm far from that.

HERMES.
> I'll waste no more words. I've treated you
> Respectfully, generously – and failed.
> You're like a newly broken colt
1010   Wrestling the reins, bolting, bucking the bit.
> So clever! So confident! So weak! Mistake
> Self-confidence for wisdom, you'll fall.
> You won't be persuaded? Listen then:
> This storm, this sea of suffering,
> You call down on yourself. No hiding.
> First, our father's thunderbolt

Will split this mountain, splinter it.
Rock-tomb, rock-womb. You'll lie engulfed
For an eternity. When you do see light again,   1020
Spewed to the surface, Zeus' hunting hound,
His eagle, blood-beaked, ravenous, will strip
Your flesh, tear titbits from your liver.
Day after day after day:
A feast of agony; no end
Till some other god accepts your pain,
For your sake visiting the darks
Of Hades, gulfs of Tartarus below.
Take thought for that. I spin no idle threats.   1030
Mouthpiece of Zeus. Exact. He speaks; it is.
Look round you. Think.
D'you still put stubbornness
Ahead of common sense?

CHORUS LEADER.
Good advice, Prometheus.
Give up your anger, seek out common sense.
Do as he says.
You're wise. You're wrong. Give way.

PROMETHEUS.
No word he yaps is new to me.   1040
I'm at war, I'm wounded: no disgrace.
Let Zeus hurl lightning-spears,
Rockets, knives of fire.
Shake air, tear sky,
Tornadoes splinter Earth,
Uproot, convulse.
Boil sea, dissolve the stars.
Lift me, break me, hurl me,   1050
Black deeps of Tartarus,
Whirlwinds of fate.
Do all he likes, I'll never die.

HERMES.
Mad thoughts, mad words.
Slip rein, hard galloping,
Insanity's race is run.

To the CHORUS.

> You pity him, show sympathy.
> 1060 Go! Now. Stay here,
> Thunder-bellows, too,
> Will stone your wits away.

CHORUS LEADER.

> Try another tune! New words!
> Not this advice. You tempt,
> You preach disloyalty.
> How dare you? We stay,
> We bear what he bears.
> 1070 This we know, we learned from him:
> We spit on those who betray their friends.

HERMES.

> Remember, then, I warned you.
> Don't snarl at the fate that traps you.
> Zeus is not to blame:
> You chose it. No secret.
> You knew,
> You saw Fate's net, and jumped at it.

Exit.

PROMETHEUS.

> 1080 No more words. It's happening.
> Earth writhes.
> Thunder bellows from the deep.
> Fire-tendrils, lightning-flares.
> Hurricanes hug dust,
> Death-dervish-dance.
> Wind leaps on wind,
> Howling, tearing.
> Sky drinks sea.
> Zeus did this. His storm.
> 1090 Themis, mother!
> Sky-wheel that turns the stars!
> See how unjust my suffering.

NOTES

Persians

1 'Helle's gulf' is the Hellespont. Greek myth named it after
Helle, sister of Prince Athamas of Boeotia. When the gods
ordered Athamas' father to sacrifice the young prince, Zeus
sent a golden ram to rescue him. Athamas and Helle flew on
the ram's back from Boeotia towards Colchis; but on the way
Helle lost her grip, fell off and drowned in the water later
named after her. It was this passage that Xerxes bridged with
boats, lashing them side-by-side and building a road on top
for his army to march across. The word we translate as 'cable-
stitched' is literally 'flax-bound', and refers to the cables
which held the ships across the strait to support the roadway.
Aeschylus' description of the road as a yoke picks up another
traditional name for the Hellespont, the 'neck'.

2 This is both a straightforward reminder of Xerxes' wealth,
and a reference to the foundation-myth of the Persian people.
In this, their ancestor was Perseus, the hero born to Danae
after Zeus visited her in a shower of golden rain.

3 The Queen here uses the colloquial word by which Greeks
described outsiders (especially Persians): *barbaroi*, 'those
who say "bar-bar"'. To ancient Athenian ears, the word may
have had similar connotations to those of 'non-white' in 20th-
century racist societies. An even more bizarre – or telling –
use of the word is at the end of the Messenger's first speech,
page 10.

4 At Marathon.

5 This refers to the silver mines at Laurium, not far from Cape
Sunium. A particularly rich seam was discovered in the
mid-480s BC, and the Athenians used it to finance the
building of the fleet which fought at Salamis.

6 Granted the possibility that Aeschylus had himself been at
Salamis, and the certainty that many of his audience had
fought there, it seems likely that this is the actual warcry
used. The last line of our translation echoes Browning's
version, in *Balaustion's Adventure*.

7 Herodotus, in his description of the battle, gives credit for this success to one Ameinias of Pallene - and some scholars, knowing that Aeschylus had a brother called Ameinias, suggest that it may have been the same man.

8 Some authorities say that this group of nobles, on the small wooded island of Psytallea, included three of Xerxes' own sons. To the Persians, the death of such princes would be like the loss of gods.

9 This entrance, as the Queen's words make clear, contrasts with her earlier appearance (line 155). There, she was dressed in all her royal finery, was surrounded by attendants (and, some say, rode in a chariot). Here she is alone, dressed in mourning, and on foot. The 'mirror' effect of the two scenes, psychological and dramatic, is marked.

10 'Majesty of Death' is Hades, Zeus' brother, king of the Underworld. Wherever possible, the Greeks avoided speaking his name directly or showing him in paintings, sculptures or other art.

11 No evidence survives about how this was done in the Greek theatre. Scholars agree that it was unlikely that the Ghost simply walked on – as Clytemnestra's ghost seems to do in *Eumenides*. There are various suggestions: that the Ghost appeared on the roof of the stage building, or from behind wheeled screens which were pulled away, or from an underground passage. Implausible as it may seem, the last explanation is most likely, and is even supported by (sketchy) archaeological evidence.

12 These prophecies of disaster, perhaps given to Darius, may have formed part of one of the earlier plays in the trilogy, now lost.

13 Mardus was a pretender, a Median prince who usurped the Persian throne. Seven conspirators, led by Artaphrenes and including Darius, overthrew him and killed him. They then cast lots for kingship, and Darius won.

14 This refers to the Battle of Plataea, fought on the Boeotian plain beside the river Asopus in 479BC. Xerxes' brother-in-law Mardonius led the huge Persian land-force (left high and dry in Greece after the naval defeat at Salamis the year before), and lost.

15 The metaphor is Aeschylus' own, and refers either to pitch bubbling from the ground, or to black water bubbling from the depths of a marsh. Events during the Gulf War of 1991, as we wrote this translation, gave the metaphor even more immediate, more sinister force.

16 From here to the end of the play, lyric lamentation fills the stage – as hard to reconstruct from the words alone as the last act of an opera would be without music or *mise-en-scène*.

Seven Against Thebes

17 Most scholars hold that these Citizens are not the same people as the Chorus. In most surviving Greek plays, the Chorus has an entrance-ode, like the one which begins here at line 78. Apart from this play, only Sophocles' *King Oedipus* opens with a group of silent people waiting to hear what the king has to say. Some editors believe, by contrast, that there were no extras onstage at all, and that Eteocles made his opening speech to the audience, 'casting' them as the people of Thebes.

18 In Greek, the metre of the entrance-ode which follows is jerky and unpredictable, reflecting abrupt changes in the flow of thought and imagery. This suggests that the Chorus may have entered in disorder, distracted movements matching the panic in their words: a spectacular effect, achieved by the simplest means.

19 E!, here and elsewhere, is direct transliteration of the Greek: a short, gasping sound, like the 'e' in 'hen'.

20 The founding myth of Thebes tells how Cadmus, watering his cattle, was attacked by a monstrous snake, a creature from the Underworld. He killed it and sowed its teeth in the ground – and armed warriors grew like corn. They fought each other until only five were left. These five swore allegiance to Cadmus and helped him to build a new city: Thebes. They were revered ever afterwards as the 'Sown Men', ancestors of the Theban people.

21 The English *double-entendre* matches the Greek. Our 'maiden store' stands for the Greek word for 'rowing bench', used in a similar way of Cassandra in *Agamemnon*, and of a ferryman's wife in Aristophanes' *Ecclesiazusae*.

22 From here to the end, the Greek is a salad of original lines, additions, alterations and guesses, some dating back almost to Aeschylus' own lifetime: see also notes 23, 24, 25. There may have been a Messenger's speech longer than the abrupt announcement which survives: perhaps a description of the duel between the brothers. Our translation, from here to the end of the play, follows Page's edition, but not slavishly.

23 Some editors treat the next dozen lines as spurious, a post-Aeschylean addition to put Antigone and Ismene into the play (perhaps after the success of Sophocles' *Antigone* in 441BC). The problems are (1) that to end the trilogy with prophecies about the brothers' burial seems less satisfactory than lamenting their death, and (2) that many of the lines which survive (especially 1005 onwards) are in a style markedly different from anything else which survives by Aeschylus. The dozen lines here, and the characters Antigone and Ismene, can be omitted without damage to the play. See notes 24, 25.

24 Following Page's edition, we give the antiphonal section which follows to Antigone and Ismene. If they are omitted from the performance, the lines can be spoken by two antiphonal groups of the Chorus.

25 From here to the end of the play, the style is so different that most scholars say that the lines must be by someone else. Aeschylus' original play (and the trilogy of which it was the final part) may have ended at this point with a choral exit-ode, now lost. (The surviving exit-ode, 1054ff, is both inconclusive and unAeschylean: bathos of two kinds at once.)

Suppliants

26 There is scholarly debate about whether Danaus enters with the Chorus, or later (line 176). The entry of the Chorus also raises, for the first time, the question of numbers which recurs throughout the play. Are all 50 Danaids present, or merely a representative number? See also notes 32, 33, 34.

27 In myth, Procne's husband Tereus raped her sister Philomela, and Procne punished him by killing their son Itys and serving him in a stew for his father. The gods changed

the survivors into birds: Tereus into a hoopoe, Philomela into a swallow and Procne into a nightingale, forever lamenting. The nightingale was a symbol for sorrow throughout Greek literature; Aeschylus himself used it again in the Cassandra scene of *Agamemnon*.

28 This refers to Epaphus, the child born after Zeus, disguised as a bull, mated with Io in the cow-shape imposed on her by Hera. Epaphus, worshipped in Egypt as the bull-god Apis, was in Greek myth the father of Libya (mother of Danaus and Aegyptus): hence the Danaids' claim here that Zeus their ancestor should help them.

29 There is confusion here. In myth, the Argive king's name is Gelanor, 'Earth-lord'. But the text here means, literally, 'I am the Pelasgian sinew of the Ancient Earthborn', and this led some editors to name the king Pelasgus. (In myth, however, Pelasgus was Mother Earth's son, the first human being ever to exist; he had no connection with Argos.) We have followed the original manuscripts, and given the king no name at all.

30 Although little is known of Greek theatrical dance, scholars suggest that the section which follows may have been accompanied by a dance enactment of Io's wanderings and her release from suffering at the hand of Zeus. For her story, see note 40.

31 With the appearance of the Egyptian, grammar and syntax go haywire, as if language itself collapses under the weight of the Chorus' panic and the Egyptian's rage. Where non-verbal sounds are in the Greek, we give them phonetically and exactly. We have mirrored the fractured syntax of the Greek, and also the way, as the scene proceeds, the Egyptian's speeches become ever more formal, more organised, and the Chorus' utterances do not. As might be expected, lack of coherent syntax puzzled early copyists and editors, so that surviving manuscripts are a mess of rationalisations, guesses and mistakes. Even the distribution of speakers is doubtful. We follow Page's edition, with occasional guesses, rationalisations (and no doubt mistakes) of our own.

32 This entry poses more problems about numbers onstage. Some editors, having already claimed that the Egyptian is

accompanied by sailors, now say that the Argive king comes in with soldiers. It was not uncommon in Greek theatre for extras to 'dress' the stage, like spear-carriers in Shakespeare – but the numbers here, particularly added to a Chorus of perhaps 50 Danaids, are high.

33 At this point, number problems get out of hand. If there were 50 daughters in the Chorus, each with her own servant, that means a group of 100 people – beyond the purse of most backers, and out of keeping with what little we know of 5th-century Greek production style. Some editors suggest that the lines are spurious, from a later, more epic revival. But it is just as easy to assume that there never were 50 daughters, or 50 maids, onstage at all: the standard Chorus of 12 or 15, and a (perhaps smaller) group of extras playing maids, stood for all.

34 The problems here are almost insoluble. The Greek gives no indication who is onstage, or who speaks each group of lines. The content of the lines suggests conflict, between at least two opinions. Some editors divide the lines between two groups of the Chorus; others imagine a new group altogether, of Argive women. Our 'solution' derives from the dramatic situation and the logic of the lines, both of which suggest not resolution but tension (perhaps looking forward to the later, lost, plays in the trilogy).

Prometheus Bound

35 The problems of staging *Prometheus Bound*, which have engaged scholars and theatre people almost since the play was written, begin with this scene. Is Prometheus, as the lines suggest, literally fastened to the 'rock' – and if so, how? Some writers, concerned that lack of movement would be a serious restraint on the actor, and would increase the already static nature of the play, have suggested that he was merely shackled, and that his chains allowed some movement. Others, taking literally words like 'peg' and 'spike', and such lines as 64-65 (the 'beak of steel' which foreshadows the beak of Zeus' eagle) suggest that one way to stage the scene was for Might and Force to bring in not a pinioned actor but a huge wickerwork figure, inside which the actor could crawl once the pegging was complete. This could have been spectacular,

but it could also have been ludicrous – and there are few other 'lay figures' in extant Greek drama, and none which require an actor to crawl inside.

36 The text here has suggested to some scholars that the Chorus made its entrance in a winged chariot – or even, in the wilder moments of desk-bound fantasy, in one winged chariot each. If a single chariot were used, its weight, coupled with that of the chorus-actors, would have been over two tonnes: unlikely if not impracticable. It seems more plausible that the Chorus entered in the normal way, on the ground, and that ideas of flying and of 'stepping down' from Sky to Earth were left to the audience's imagination, or were cues for dance.

37 The lines suggest that Ocean enters riding a winged sea-creature. This would have been possible using the theatre crane, and is an effect parallelled in other surviving plays (for example Aristophanes' *Peace*, in which the leading actor 'rides' from ground level to stage-building roof on a giant dung-beetle). There is no evidence for or against – and in any case theatres varied in size, and not all of them (archaeology suggests) were equipped with cranes.

38 In myth, Typhon (or Typhoeus) was a hundred-headed giant, the child of Mother Earth and Tartarus. Enraged by the gods' defeat of his brother-giants, he clambered up to attack Olympus, and Zeus blasted him with a thunderbolt, hurling him from Olympus to Earth, and piled Mount Etna on top to pin him down. Some scholars suggest that the version of *Prometheus Bound* we have may be a revision made for performance in Sicily – and that this passage about Typhon may have been written into the script to please local audiences. There is no evidence either way. In some versions of the myth, Typhon was the father (and the sea-monster Echidna the mother) of the gryphon (dog/eagle or dog/vulture) which Zeus sent to feast on Prometheus' liver.

39 In myth, Hesione was a daughter of Ocean (and therefore a half-sister of the Chorus of this play). She was not the same person as Laomedon's daughter Hesione, whom Heracles saved from a sea-monster.

40 Io, in myth, was the daughter of the river-god Inachus. Zeus seduced her, and Hera punished her by changing her into a

cow and sending hundred-eyed (or, in Aeschylus' version,
ten-thousand-eyed) Argus to drive her in exile across the
world. Heracles killed Argus, and Hera rescued his eyes,
placing them in the tail of the peacock. She sent a gadfly to
sting Io into madness, continuing her wandering. It is during
these wanderings that Aeschylus imagines Io coming on
Prometheus. Some writers say that the whole Io section of the
play is an interpolation, nothing to do with the story. But its
language, especially Prometheus' narrative of Io's wanderings, is as sweeping and grand as anything Aeschylus ever
wrote, and the scene must have been spectacular, with Io's
restless dancing set against Prometheus' pinioned majesty.
The Io myth continues (as Prometheus in this play proph-
esies) with her arrival in Egypt, where Zeus restores her to
sanity and human shape, and she becomes an ancestor of the
first royal Egyptian dynasty.

41 This refers to Heracles, whose mother Alcmena, in myth,
was descended from Io's daughter Libya. According to the
myth, Zeus finally forgave the Titans and set them free,
whereupon Prometheus told him the secret which he had
been keeping – namely that if Zeus married Thetis she would
bear a son greater than his father. In gratitude, Zeus sent
Heracles to kill the gryphon which was tearing Prometheus'
liver, and Prometheus was at last set free. Aeschylus' lost
play *Prometheus Freed* may have covered much of this story:
see Introduction, page xxxi.

Our main Greek text throughout was Page's Oxford edition of
1972, and we also used several earlier editions and commen-
taries, notably that of H J Rose. Among general books on Greek
drama, we found much of interest in Webster's *Greek Theatre
Production*, Lawler's *The Dance of the Ancient Theatre* and
Herington's *Aeschylus*, and we also recommend three specialist
books: Taplin's *The Stagecraft of Aeschylus*, Garvie's *Aeschylus'
Supplices: Play and Trilogy*, and Griffith's *The Authenticity of
Prometheus Bound*. On many controversial matters, however, we
made up our own minds: it would be unfair for any of these
scholars to shoulder blame.

A Note on the Translators and Series Editor

FREDERIC RAPHAEL is the author of three volumes of short stories, 16 novels including *The Limits of Love*, *April, June and November* and *Heaven and Earth*. His screenplays include the Oscar-winning *Darling*, and his work for television includes *The Glittering Prizes* and *After the War*. His translations with Kenneth McLeish include not only this version of Aeschylus, but also plays by Euripides and the complete poems of Catullus.

KENNETH MCLEISH'S books include *The Theatre of Aristophanes*, *Shakespeare's People A-Z* and *The Good Reading Guide*. His translations include plays by all the extant Greek and Roman dramatists, and by Ibsen, Feydeau, Labiche and Goldoni. His translation of Sophocles' *Electra* was directed by Deborah Warner at the RSC in 1989, and his version of Ibsen's *Peer Gynt* was directed by Declan Donnellan at the Royal National Theatre in 1990.

J MICHAEL WALTON worked in the professional theatre as an actor and director before joining the University of Hull, where he is Reader in Theatre History in the Drama Department. He has published three books on Greek theatre, *Greek Theatre Practice*, *The Greek Sense of Theatre: Tragedy Reviewed*, and *Living Greek Theatre: A Handbook of Classical Performance and Modern Production*. He has also published in a number of areas of more modern British and European theatre, is the editor of *Craig on Theatre* and General Editor of Methuen Classical Drama in Translation.